The Step By Step Guide To Become Unf**kwithable

The Key To Creating A Life That You Love

Coach Michael Taylor

Published by Creation Publishing Group LLC

www.creationpublishing.com

© 2024 Michael Taylor

ISBN # 979-8-9857286-9-9

Library of Congress Control Number # 2024906555

Published and printed in the United States of America.

Table of Contents

Acknowledgements

First, foremost, and always, I must acknowledge the Divine Intelligence that created and is still creating this amazing Universe we live in. I recognize this Intelligence as the source of my creativity and inspiration for writing this book (with a little help from ChatGPT) and I am eternally grateful for the gift of writing bestowed upon me by this Intelligence. I am constantly amazed how effortless writing has become for me (as an author of 14 books) and I understand that writing is a gift and it is to be used to share the lessons and experiences I've had which allowed me to overcome a host of adversities and challenges in my life. I'm reminded of this famous quote; "who I am is God's gift to me, what I make of myself is my gift to God." This book is my way of thanking God for giving me the gift of writing.

It's important for me to acknowledge Dr. Wayne Dyer for being my favorite mentor and spiritual teacher. I began reading his works more than 30 years ago and his wisdom is primarily responsible for how I think and how I view being human. I am forever indebted to Dr. Dyer for teaching me how to think and to embrace the idea that I am a spiritual being having a human experience, not just a human being having a spiritual experience.

Albert Einstein has also had a huge impact on how I view the world. I love how he combined science with spirituality without the dogma or doctrine of organized religion. His wisdom and teachings have always inspired me to think deeply and challenge everything with critical thinking. He is by far my all-time favorite scientist and thought leader.

I recently partnered with George Shephard of 360 Summits to host an online summit. During one of our calls, I mentioned the word "unf**kwithable" which I learned from Vishen Lakhiani, and George immediately mentioned I should write a book about it. He then challenged me to write the book and this book is the result of that conversation. He agreed to write the forward for the book and I'm looking forward to partnering with him to not only launch my summit, but to also market this book. I'm really looking forward to building a business relationship with him. So, here's a shoutout to George, I'm really looking forward to our upcoming collaborations.

I must give credit to my mom Geneva for instilling a sense of optimism and infinite possibilities in me at a very early age. Her greatest lesson she taught me was, "if you want something badly enough, there is no one or no thing that can keep you from attaining it except yourself". Everything I am, I owe to her. I love you mom!

Last but definitely not least, I must acknowledge my amazing wife Bedra who is my biggest cheerleader and greatest supporter. She believes in me as much as I believe in myself and I absolutely love having her as my life partner. She is without question the coolest wife ever, and I am truly blessed to be able to share life with her. I love you Mrs. B! I told you, you won the lottery!

Foreword

by George Shephard
www.360summits.com

In a time where it's not just fashionable to embrace 3 gender restrooms, snowflakes, manbuns, and no child left behind... Unfortunately, in the sprint for inclusion, we have left behind the ONE thing that defined the greatest success stories in history.

You guessed it... Becoming Un-Fuckwith-able.

Being UFWA doesn't mean you have to get a teardrop tattoo on your cheek or adorn yourself with jewelry or firearms, it's a state of mind that ultimately expands your energy field to be felt (or observed) by all those around you - both strangers and pals.

The UFWA man or woman is a magnet for opportunity and experiences for personal growth that can create an EPIC life that even inspires the snowflakes to become more than what society has programmed them to be.

Do you know what the most powerful force on earth is...?

Water.

It has the power to carve valleys and canyons out of solid stone, to transform mountains into grains of sand and when mixed with raw earth it can bury a civilization or be formed by the hands of an artist into a useful (and valuable) vessel that can last for centuries.

Melt enough snowflakes and you can have a powerful ocean of raw kinetic potential energy waiting to be unleashed into the world.

You have the power to change the face of your own life and the culture that surrounds it!

Don't like your circumstances…? Become UFWA and you can change it.

Don't like your environment…? Become UFWA and you can rise above it.

The relationship with your spouse not fulfilling you…? Become UFWA and breathe life into a stale or dying partnership.

This is the point where some people will tell you… it's NOT YOUR FAULT!

That's not me. If you continue to let the world around you continue to FW you, then the outcomes, circumstances and the future of your life will forever be dictated by others.

In essence you voluntarily become a slave on the plantation, building everyone else's dreams but your own.

You voluntarily check yourself into a prison in which escape can be damn near impossible. Right now, the other inmates are sizing you up to make you their "bitch". Is that how you envisioned your life?

It's time for your ocean of RAW, focused UN-FUCKWITH-ABLE energy to crash against the mountain, break the shackles of servitude and unlock your MF prison cell so you can step into your FULL potential!

No one is going to do it for you. This is one thing you MUST do for yourself and all those who depend on you… and this book will show you how.

Introduction

In his groundbreaking, New York Times bestselling book, The Code of The Extraordinary Mind, Vishen Lakhiani introduced me to the word, "unfuckwithable". While some people may be offended by the vulgarity, I think it is the perfect word to describe the feeling we can get when we invest in our own potential and discover who we really are. As soon as I read the word, I realized it summarized how I feel most of the time as a result of the inner work of transformation I've done over the past 25 years. Some people may use the word invincible, indestructible, unbeatable, unconquerable, or indomitable, but these words do not pack the same punch as "unfuckwithable". I remember a time in my life when I was a people pleasing nice guy who had an insatiable need for other people's approval who lacked self-confidence and was filled with toxic shame. And now, I can honestly say, I feel unfuckwithable the majority of the time.

Getting to this point in my life wasn't easy. It began with me losing everything through divorce, bankruptcy, foreclosure, depression, and homelessness. These adversities challenged me to began my inner journey of transformation, and I've been on this journey for more than 30 years. As a result of going on this journey, I was able to rebuild my life and now I'm living my version of an extraordinary one.

I am convinced that every human being has the capacity to build extraordinary lives. What is needed are some tools of awareness to help guide them on their journey. This book is one such tool. I firmly believe if the reader incorporates the wisdom from this book into their lives, their lives can become extraordinary. There is a small caveat to this claim, it is simple, but not easy.

We live in a world that promotes instant gratification and quick fixes, it's important to understand that this does not apply to transformation. Transformation isn't easy! As a matter of fact, it can be difficult and painful. But rest assured that the joy you can experience after committing to your transformation will be worth it.

At a time when it appears that the world is falling apart, I will assert that I believe there has never been a better time to be alive on the planet than right now. By the time you complete this book, there is a good chance that you might begin believing the same thing. If you begin your inner journey of transformation and discover who you truly are, you too will become "unfuckwithable" and nothing will be impossible for you.

Good luck!

Michael "Happy Ass" Taylor

The ultimate measure of a man is not where he stands in moments of comfort and convenience, but where he stands at times of challenge and controversy.
— Dr. Martin Luther King Jr.

CHAPTER 1

Adversity Is Your Ally

Embracing Adversity as a Friend

Adversity, often viewed as an unwelcome guest in our lives, has a way of showing up uninvited and disrupting our carefully laid plans. It can be overwhelming, causing stress, anxiety, and a sense of helplessness. However, what if we were to shift our perspective and see adversity not as an enemy to be defeated, but as a friend sent to teach us valuable lessons?

Embracing adversity as a friend requires a shift in mindset and a willingness to embrace discomfort. Instead of resisting challenges, we can choose to lean into them, recognizing that they offer opportunities for growth and self-discovery. Adversity can be a powerful catalyst for transformation, pushing us out of our comfort zones and challenging us to rise above our limitations.

When we embrace adversity as a friend, we open ourselves up to the possibility of learning valuable lessons and gaining new insights. We begin to see challenges as stepping stones on the path to personal development and success, rather than insurmountable obstacles.

By changing our perspective on adversity, we can cultivate resilience and strength in the face of life's challenges. We learn to adapt, evolve, and grow through adversity, developing a deeper sense of self-awareness and self-confidence.

Embracing adversity as a friend is not about denying the difficulties we face or pretending that everything is fine. It is about acknowledging the reality of our circumstances while choosing to respond with courage, resilience, and an open heart.

When we embrace adversity as a friend, we tap into our inner strength and resourcefulness. We discover that we are capable of overcoming even the most daunting challenges and that we have the power to shape our own destiny.

In the end, embracing adversity as a friend is a powerful act of self-love and self-empowerment. By facing challenges head-on and embracing the lessons they have to offer, we can transform ourselves and our lives in ways we never thought possible.

As we navigate the twists and turns of life, it is important to remember that adversity is not our enemy but a guide and teacher. It is through facing challenges and overcoming obstacles that we truly discover our strength and resilience. So, let us welcome adversity with open arms, knowing that it is through these trials that we can unlock our fullest potential and emerge stronger and wiser than before.

Embracing adversity as a friend also teaches us the value of perseverance and endurance. In facing adversity head-on, we develop a resilience that allows us to weather life's storms with grace and dignity. We learn to trust in our ability to overcome challenges, knowing that each struggle is an opportunity for growth and self-improvement.

Furthermore, embracing adversity as a friend can lead us to a deeper understanding of ourselves and our place in the world. Through the trials and tribulations we face, we uncover hidden strengths and talents that we may not have known existed. Adversity becomes a canvas on which we paint our resilience and determination, creating a work of art that embodies the essence of our true selves.

Ultimately, by embracing adversity as a friend, we shift our perspective from one of fear and resistance to one of acceptance and growth. We come to see challenges not as roadblocks but as signposts pointing us towards greater self-awareness and personal fulfillment. In this way, adversity becomes not something to be avoided or feared, but a welcomed companion on our journey towards becoming the best version of ourselves.

Finding The Hidden Gems in Challenges

In the labyrinth of life, challenges often present themselves, serving as gateways to personal evolution and self-discovery. It is in the crucible of adversity that our truest strengths are revealed, and the depths of our resilience are tested.

Obstacles, though daunting at first glance, hold within them the potential for growth and transformation. They shape us, mold us, and push us beyond the confines of our comfort zones. It is through facing these challenges head-on that we uncover hidden reservoirs of courage and fortitude, propelling us forward on our journey of self-discovery.

In the face of a challenge, it is natural to feel a sense of resistance or fear. However, by embracing the discomfort and uncertainty that challenges bring, we open ourselves up to a world of possibilities and opportunities for learning. Each obstacle is a teacher in disguise, offering us invaluable lessons that can shape our character and enrich our understanding of the world around us.

Moreover, challenges provide us with a canvas on which to paint our most authentic selves. They compel us to tap into our creativity, problem-solving skills, and resourcefulness, driving us to explore new horizons and push the boundaries of what we thought possible. In over-coming challenges, we not only discover our inner strengths but also our capacity for innovation and adaptability.

As we navigate the twists and turns of life's challenges, we must re-member that beneath the surface lies a treasure trove of hidden gems waiting to be unearthed. These gems, in the form of resilience, wisdom, and personal growth, are the rewards that come from facing our chal-lenges with courage and a willingness to learn.

The journey of self-discovery is not a linear path but rather a spi-raling ascent towards higher truths and deeper self-awareness. Each challenge met and conquered is a stepping stone on this path, guiding us towards a more profound understanding of ourselves and the world around us. It is through these challenges that we come to realize our limitless potential and the boundless depths of our inner strength.

In embracing challenges, we are reminded of the impermanence of life and the constant flux of the universe. Every obstacle we face serves as a reminder of our resilience and adaptability in the face of change. By leaning into the discomfort and uncertainty that challenges bring, we cultivate a sense of inner peace and acceptance, knowing that we have the power to overcome whatever adversity comes our way.

Ultimately, challenges are not barriers to our growth but rather cat-alysts for transformation and renewal. They push us to question our assumptions, expand our horizons, and redefine our limitations. By welcoming challenges with an open heart and a curious mind, we open ourselves up to a world of endless possibilities and profound personal growth.

The Power of Resilience and Persistence

In the intricate tapestry of life, resilience and persistence serve as the threads that weave together the profound essence of human strength and fortitude. As we navigate the unpredictable currents of existence, challenges inevitably arise, testing the very fabric of our being. It is in these moments of adversity that the true mettle of one's character is revealed.

Resilience, like a mighty oak tree swaying in the face of a fierce storm, embodies the ability to bend without breaking. It is the steel core within us that enables us to weather the harshest of circumstances and emerge stronger on the other side. Cultivating resilience requires a deep-rooted sense of self-awareness and an unwavering belief in our capacity to overcome obstacles. It beckons us to embrace change and uncertainty with an open heart, knowing that every trial we face is an opportunity for growth and transformation.

Persistence, akin to a steady flame that refuses to be extinguished, fuels the fire of our aspirations and propels us forward in the pursuit of our dreams. It is the relentless force that drives us to keep pushing beyond our limits, even when the path ahead seems daunting and insurmountable. True persistence demands unwavering dedication and a willingness to endure hardships with unwavering determination. It is the beacon that guides us through the darkest of nights, reminding us that success is not measured by the absence of obstacles but by the unwavering resolve to overcome them.

As we embrace the intertwined virtues of resilience and persistence, we illuminate the path to our highest potential and unlock the boundless power within us. In the crucible of life's challenges, we are forged into beings of strength and resilience, capable of weathering any storm and rising triumphant in the face of adversity. It is through the alchemy of struggle and perseverance that we discover the true depth of our courage and the limitless potential of the human spirit.

Beyond the surface manifestations of resilience and persistence lies a deeper understanding of the interconnected nature of these virtues.

Resilience, it is said, is not merely the ability to bounce back from set-backs but also the capacity to adapt and grow in the face of adversity. It is a dynamic force that enables us to embrace change and uncertainty with grace and resilience, knowing that every challenge we encounter is an opportunity for self-discovery and transformation.

Similarly, persistence is not merely the act of relentless pursuit of our goals but also the unwavering commitment to our dreams and aspirations. It is the unwavering faith in our own capabilities and the courage to keep moving forward despite the obstacles that stand in our way. True persistence requires a deep reservoir of inner strength and determination, a steadfast resolve to persevere even when the odds seem insurmountable.

In the dance of resilience and persistence, we find a profound synergy that propels us towards our highest potential. Like yin and yang, these virtues complement and balance each other, guiding us through the ebbs and flows of life with unwavering grace and courage. It is through the harmonious interplay of resilience and persistence that we uncover the true essence of our being and realize the limitless power that resides within us.

As we journey through the labyrinth of life, let us remember that in every challenge we face, we are given an opportunity to cultivate resilience and embrace persistence. Let us harness the transformative power of these virtues to navigate the complexities of existence with courage and grace, knowing that within us lies the strength to overcome any obstacle and the resilience to emerge triumphant in the face of adversity.

Turning Setbacks into Stepping Stones

In the turbulent seas of life, setbacks stand as formidable waves that test the resilience and fortitude of our spirit. They are the unforeseen obstacles that emerge in the midst of our journey, challenging our resolve and pushing us to navigate uncharted territories of adversity. How we confront and grow from these setbacks molds the strength of our character and shapes the trajectory of our destiny.

Setbacks manifest in multifaceted forms, each carrying its unique blend of obstacles and opportunities for introspection. Whether it be a professional setback that derails our career aspirations, a personal disappointment that shakes the foundations of our identity, a fractured relationship that leaves us emotionally raw, or a health crisis that prompts us to reevaluate our mortality, setbacks compel us to confront the fragility of our existence and compel us to reassess the paths we have chosen.

Embracing setbacks as indispensable stepping stones on the path to personal and professional evolution necessitates a paradigm shift in perspective. It mandates a willingness to embrace discomfort, uncertainty, and failure as essential components of the metamorphosis towards self-actualization. Rather than perceiving setbacks through a lens of defeat, they can be seen as profound catalysts for growth, resilience, and self-discovery.

At the core of transforming setbacks into stepping stones lies the transformative power of resilience. Resilience acts as the anchor that steadies us amidst turbulent waters, enabling us to rebound from adversity with grace, wisdom, and fortitude. Cultivating resilience demands a deep well of self-awareness, emotional intelligence, and inner strength, empowering us to weather the tempests of life with unwavering resolve and unwavering faith in our intrinsic capabilities.

In the face of setbacks, cultivating self-compassion and prioritizing self-care are essential practices. Acknowledge the full spectrum of your emotions – embrace the depths of disappointment, anger, or sadness, but also extend compassion and kindness towards yourself. Understand that setbacks do not define your worth or your potential; rather, they serve as temporary crossroads that challenge you to summon the depths of your resilience and courage.

Setbacks, far from signaling defeat, encompass within them seeds of unparalleled growth and transformation. By reframing setbacks as invaluable opportunities for introspection, learning, and self-improvement, we harness their potent alchemy, metamorphosing adversity into an empowered springboard towards a future illuminated by resilience, purpose, and unwavering inner strength.

Embracing Change With Open Arms

Change is a fundamental aspect of human existence, woven into the fabric of our lives like the threads of time themselves. It is a force that shapes our circumstances, challenges our perceptions, and propels us forward on the path of self-discovery and growth. Yet, despite its omnipresence, many of us find ourselves resistant to change, clinging to the familiar and the comfortable, afraid of what lies beyond the boundaries of our known world.

But what if we were to shift our perspective, to see change not as a threat but as an opportunity, a doorway to transformation and renewal? What if we were to embrace change with open hearts and open minds, welcoming it as a catalyst for personal evolution and self-realization?

Embracing change requires a willingness to let go of control, to surrender to the ebb and flow of life with trust and acceptance. It demands a courage to face the unknown, to venture into uncharted territories with faith in our own resilience and adaptability. It beckons us to release our attachment to the past and the future, to anchor ourselves firmly in the present moment where change unfolds, inviting us to dance with its rhythm and flow.

Just as the caterpillar must undergo metamorphosis within the cocoon to emerge as a butterfly, we too must undergo our own inner transformation, shedding old beliefs, patterns, and identities to step into the fullness of our potential. Change is not an enemy to be feared but a friend to be embraced, a mirror reflecting back to us the depths of our own inner strength and wisdom.

So, let us welcome change as a sacred gift, a sacred teacher, guiding us on a journey of self-discovery and self-realization. Let us trust in the inherent wisdom of the universe, in the divine orchestration of our lives, and in the infinite possibilities that lie beyond the horizon of our imagination. In the embrace of change, we find not only the courage to let go but also the magic of new beginnings, the alchemy of transformation, and the beauty of becoming who we are truly meant to be.

Change, in its essence, is the ultimate unraveling of our innermost selves, inviting us to confront our fears, embrace our vulnerabilities, and awaken to the boundless potential that resides within us. It is a mirror held up to our souls, reflecting back the truths we often seek to ignore – the impermanence of all things, the fluidity of life's currents, and the inevitability of growth through discomfort. Embracing change is a profound act of self-love, a declaration of trust in the natural order of things, and a surrender to the divine intelligence that guides us on our journey through the unknown.

As we navigate the uncharted waters of change, let us remember that we are not alone in this process. We are supported by the unseen forces of the universe, by the gentle whispers of our intuition, and by the guiding light of our own inner wisdom. In the midst of uncertainty and upheaval, we can find solace in the knowing that change is not a force to be conquered but a sacred dance to be embraced, leading us ever closer to the essence of our true selves.

Transforming Fear into Fuel For Success

Fear, an intricate emotion deeply ingrained in the human psyche, possesses the ability to shape our perceptions, decisions, and ultimately our destinies. It is a primal instinct that has evolved over millennia to protect us from imminent danger, triggering a cascade of responses that prime our bodies for fight, flight, or freeze. However, in the complexities of modern society, fear can often manifest as a shadow that looms over our aspirations, leading us to shrink back from challenges and opportunities that could lead to growth and fulfillment.

Within the realm of fear lies a duality that mirrors our innermost vulnerabilities and strengths. Inherent fears, such as the fear of mortality or physical harm, are deeply rooted in our survival instincts, serving as a necessary mechanism to navigate the dangers of the world. These primal fears are hardwired into our biology, compelling us to seek safety and security in the face of perceived threats.

On the other hand, learned fears are a product of our experiences, upbringing, and societal conditioning. These fears are shaped by our past traumas, negative beliefs, and cultural narratives that imprint upon our psyches, creating barriers that inhibit our potential and limit our capacity for growth. From childhood onwards, we absorb messages about what is safe, acceptable, or desirable, internalizing fears that may no longer serve us as we navigate the complexities of adulthood.

To transcend the grip of fear and harness its transformative power, we must embark on an inner journey of self-discovery and self-awareness. By shining a light on the shadows of our fears, we can unravel the narratives that hold us captive and liberate ourselves from the limitations they impose. Through introspection and reflection, we can uncover the root causes of our fears, identifying the ingrained patterns and beliefs that keep us trapped in a cycle of avoidance and stagnation.

Courage, the antidote to fear, emerges as we confront our deepest fears with a spirit of openness and vulnerability. Stepping into the discomfort of uncertainty, we defy the status quo and challenge the limiting beliefs that have constrained our potential. Each act of courage becomes a beacon of light that illuminates the path to self-empowerment and growth, revealing hidden reserves of strength and resilience that we never knew existed within us.

As we navigate the labyrinth of fear and self-discovery, we cultivate a deeper understanding of ourselves and the world around us. Through the alchemy of fear, we transform adversity into opportunity, turning obstacles into stepping stones towards our highest aspirations. Embracing fear as a catalyst for growth and transformation, we unlock the door to a brighter future filled with limitless possibilities and untapped potentials waiting to be realized.

The Beauty of Growth Through Adversity

The intricacies of adversity are a profound exploration of the human spirit, delving deep into the core of our existence and unraveling the layers of resilience that define our being. In the tapestry of life, adversity weaves a complex narrative that tests the limits of our endurance and fortitude, revealing the depths of our inner strength and courage.

As we journey through the crucible of hardship, we are confronted with the raw essence of our vulnerabilities, fears, and insecurities. It is in these moments of vulnerability that we are stripped down to our most authentic selves, laying bare the intricacies of our emotions and thought patterns. Adversity acts as a mirror, reflecting back to us the aspects of ourselves that we may have overlooked or suppressed, beckoning us to confront them with honesty and acceptance.

In the dance of adversity, we are called to embrace the discomfort and uncertainty that inevitably accompany struggle. It is through this embrace that we cultivate a deeper sense of self-awareness and self-compassion, recognizing that the journey through hardship is not a linear progression but a tumultuous voyage of self-discovery. We learn to navigate the jagged terrain of adversity with grace and resilience, trusting in our own inner resources to guide us through the darkest of times.

Just as a sculptor shapes clay into a masterpiece, so too does adversity mold and sculpt us into beings of greater depth and wisdom. The fires of struggle refine us, burning away the impurities of doubt and fear, leaving behind a gleaming core of authenticity and strength. We may stumble and falter along the way, but it is through these moments of imperfection that we find the true beauty of our humanity.

As we traverse the winding road of adversity, we are reminded of the transient nature of our struggles and the impermanence of our pain. Each obstacle we face is but a stepping stone on the path to growth and transformation, a testament to our resilience and determination. In the heart of adversity lies the seed of our greatest potential, waiting to be nurtured and cultivated into a flourishing garden of self-discovery and empowerment.

In the grand tapestry of life, adversity plays a vital role in shaping the narrative of our existence. It challenges us to rise above our limitations, to embrace our vulnerabilities, and to harness the power of our inner strength. As we navigate the ebb and flow of hardship and struggle, let us remember that adversity is not a hindrance but a catalyst for growth, a mirror reflecting the brilliance and resilience that reside within each of us.

Cultivating a Positive Mindset in Tough Times

Amidst the stormy seas of life, when challenges seem insurmountable and the weight of adversity feels overwhelming, there lies a beacon of hope within each and every one of us - a positive mindset. Cultivating a positive mindset in tough times is not merely a whimsical notion, but rather a powerful tool that can see us through even the darkest of days.

It all starts with a shift in perception. Instead of allowing negative thoughts and emotions to consume us, we must consciously choose to focus on the silver linings, no matter how faint they may seem. This does not mean ignoring the difficulties we face, but rather reframing them in a way that empowers us to see opportunities for growth and learning.

Practicing gratitude is another key component of fostering a positive mindset in tough times. By taking the time to appreciate the blessings, big and small, that surround us, we can cultivate a spirit of abundance and resilience that helps us navigate the storms with grace and fortitude. Research has shown that gratitude can have a profound impact on our mental and emotional well-being, helping us shift our focus from what is lacking to what we already have.

Self-care is essential during challenging times, as it is often easy to neglect our own well-being when faced with adversity. Taking time to nourish our bodies, minds, and spirits through activities that bring us joy and peace can help us maintain a positive outlook even in the face of adversity. This can include practices such as meditation, exercise, spending time in nature, or engaging in creative pursuits that nourish our souls.

Furthermore, developing resilience in the face of tough times involves building a strong support system of friends, family, and mentors who can provide guidance, encouragement, and a listening ear when needed. Surrounding ourselves with positive influences and seeking out those who uplift us can make a significant difference in how we navigate challenges and maintain a hopeful outlook.

In today's fast-paced and ever-changing world, the ability to adapt and thrive in the face of adversity is more important than ever. Cultivating a positive mindset is not just a feel-good sentiment but a practical strategy for tackling life's challenges head-on. When we approach tough times with a positive outlook, we are better equipped to overcome obstacles, learn from our experiences, and emerge stronger on the other side.

In addition to shifting our mindset and practicing gratitude, it is also crucial to develop emotional intelligence during tough times. Emotional intelligence encompasses self-awareness, self-regulation, empathy, and social skills, all of which play a vital role in managing stress, navigating conflicts, and building strong relationships. By honing our emotional intelligence skills, we can more effectively cope with the ups and downs of life and maintain a sense of equilibrium even in the face of adversity.

Moreover, resilience - the ability to bounce back from setbacks and persevere in the face of adversity - is a key trait that can be cultivated through intentional practice. Resilient individuals are not immune to challenges, but they possess the inner strength and adaptability to weather the storms of life and emerge even stronger. Building resilience involves fostering a growth mindset, embracing failures as learning opportunities, and developing coping strategies to navigate challenging circumstances.

In conclusion, cultivating a positive mindset in tough times is a multifaceted endeavor that requires a blend of mindset shifts, gratitude practices, self-care routines, support systems, emotional intelligence, and resilience-building strategies. By embracing these principles and incorporating them into our daily lives, we can harness the power of positivity to navigate challenges with grace, resilience, and hope.

Building Inner Strength and Confidence

In the intricate tapestry of life, the cultivation of inner strength and confidence is a profound journey that resonates deeply with the essence of our human experience. In times of turmoil and uncertainty, our inner reservoir of resilience and fortitude serves as a guiding beacon to navigate the stormy seas of adversity. The crucible of challenges not only tests the mettle of our character but also unveils the hidden treasures of our soul, revealing the untapped potential that lies dormant within us.

Embarking on the path of self-discovery through self-reflection is akin to embarking on a mystical voyage into the depths of the unknown territories of our psyche. By delving fearlessly into the labyrinth of our thoughts, emotions, and beliefs, we unearth profound insights that illuminate the shadows of our doubts and fears. This introspective journey of self-awareness empowers us to embrace our vulnerabilities, acknowledge our imperfections, and embrace the full spectrum of our being with compassion and acceptance.

The tapestry of inner strength is interwoven with the threads of resilience, adaptability, and unwavering determination. As we navigate the twists and turns of life's journey, our ability to bounce back from setbacks, pivot in the face of adversity, and stand firm in the midst of chaos becomes the hallmark of our inner fortitude. It is in these moments of profound challenge that we are called upon to summon the depths of our courage, resilience, and determination to weather the storms and emerge stronger on the other side.

Moreover, the pillars of support that bolster our spirit in times of need are the cherished bonds of companionship, love, and shared humanity. Surrounding ourselves with a tribe of kindred spirits who uplift, inspire, and encourage us can be the cornerstone of our resilience and confidence. The gentle words of encouragement, the unwavering support of a loving embrace, and the shared laughter in moments of joy serve as a wellspring of strength that nourishes our soul and fortifies our resolve in the face of adversity.

Gratitude, with its transformative power to shift our perspective from scarcity to abundance, emerges as a potent elixir that nourishes our soul and sustains our spirit in times of turmoil. By cultivating a practice of gratitude, we awaken to the beauty and wonder that surrounds us, anchoring ourselves in the present moment and finding solace in the simple pleasures of life. In the bountiful harvest of gratitude, we discover the seeds of resilience, the roots of inner strength, and the blossoms of confidence that bloom and flourish even in the harshest of conditions.

As we traverse the labyrinth of life's challenges and triumphs, the journey of cultivating inner strength and confidence becomes a sacred pilgrimage of self-discovery, growth, and transformation. Through the crucible of our trials and tribulations, we forge a profound sense of self-belief, resilience, and unwavering confidence that empowers us to navigate the stormy seas of adversity with grace, courage, and unyielding resolve.

Thriving Beyond Adversity

In the intricate tapestry of life, adversity often serves as the thread that weaves through the fabric of our experiences, shaping us in profound ways. It is in the crucible of challenges that we are refined, our true strength and resilience tested, and our innermost capabilities unearthed.

Navigating through trials and tribulations, we are faced with a choice – to succumb to the weight of adversity or to transcend it, rising above like a phoenix from the ashes. This choice, though not always easy, holds the key to our growth and transformation.

Adversity, with its sharp edges and harsh realities, has a way of revealing the depths of our character and the resilience of our spirit. It pushes us to confront our fears, to embrace uncertainty, and to forge ahead despite the odds stacked against us.

As we journey through the stormy seas of life, it is essential to remember that adversity is not a sign of weakness, but a testament to our capacity for growth and evolution. It is through adversity that we learn the art of resilience, the power of perseverance, and the beauty of resilience.

The path to thriving beyond adversity is not paved with rose petals but with thorns of challenges and obstacles. Yet, it is precisely through overcoming these obstacles that we discover our true potential, our inner strength, and our ability to triumph against all odds.

So, let us embrace adversity as a catalyst for growth, a teacher of resilience, and a gateway to transformation. Let us face our challenges with grace and determination, knowing that with each trial we overcome, we emerge stronger, more resilient, and more capable of thriving beyond adversity.

In the depths of adversity lies a hidden beauty, a transformative power that transcends the immediacy of struggle. It is within the crucible of our darkest moments that we find the light of resilience, the strength to forge ahead despite the odds, and the courage to rise above the challenges that beset us.

As we navigate the tumultuous waters of life, we are tested in ways we never thought possible. The fires of adversity burn away the layers of doubt and uncertainty, revealing the core of our being – strong, resilient, and unyielding in the face of hardship.

Every trial we encounter is an opportunity for growth, a chance to learn more about ourselves and the depths of our capabilities. Adversity, though daunting and formidable, is also a transformative force, shaping us into the individuals we are destined to become.

So, let us not fear adversity, but embrace it as a teacher and a guide on our journey of self-discovery and transformation. Let us face each challenge with unwavering determination, knowing that on the other side lies a greater understanding of ourselves and a renewed sense of purpose.

"*What is arising now is not a new belief system, a new religion, spiritual ideology, or mythology. At the heart of the new consciousness lies the transcendence of thought, the newfound ability of rising above thought, of realizing a dimension within yourself that is infinitely more vast than thought. You then no longer derive your identity, your sense of who you are, from the incessant stream of thinking that in the old consciousness you take to be yourself. What a liberation to realize that the 'voice in my head' is not who I am. Who am I then? The one who sees that. The awareness that is prior to thought, the space in which the thought - or the emotion - or the sense perception - happens.*"

— Eckhart Tolle

CHAPTER 2

Awaken Your True Self

Embracing Your True Essence

The journey of self-discovery is an intricate tapestry of experiences that unveil the multidimensional layers of our true essence, calling us to embark on an introspective expedition into the depths of our being. This profound quest challenges us to transcend the superficial constructs and societal norms that have shaped our identities, urging us to delve deep into the core of our authentic selves.

As we traverse the inner landscapes of our consciousness, we encounter a myriad of emotions, thoughts, and revelations that illuminate the intricate nuances of our true nature. Each revelation serves as a mirror reflecting back to us the essence of who we truly are, shedding light on the unique gifts, talents, and virtues that lie dormant within us, waiting to be embraced and expressed.

However, amidst the revelations of our inner brilliance, we also confront the shadows of self-doubt, insecurity, and fear that lurk in the recesses of our psyche. These shadows, born out of societal conditioning and past experiences, seek to undermine our sense of worthiness and limit our potential, casting a veil of darkness over our perception of self.

Yet, it is in confronting these shadows with courage and compassion that we begin to unravel the layers of limiting beliefs and insecurities that have clouded our vision of ourselves. Through introspection and self-awareness, we embark on a journey of self-healing and self-acceptance, embracing even the most vulnerable aspects of our being with love and kindness.

Embracing our true essence is an act of radical self-love, a declaration of our inherent worthiness and deservingness of respect and acceptance. It is a journey of reclaiming our authenticity and sovereignty, allowing us to shine brightly as the unique expressions of divinity that we are, unapologetically and unconditionally.

As we embrace our true essence, we step into our power with unwavering confidence, embodying our innate wisdom and resilience as we navigate the complexities of life. This profound sense of self-empowerment enables us to live authentically and purposefully, radiating our light out into the world and inspiring others to embark on their own transformative journey of self-discovery.

Unveiling the Spiritual Being Within

As you delve deeper into the exploration of your spiritual essence, you will begin to uncover the intricate layers of your being that have been shaped by your experiences, beliefs, and perceptions. These layers, often formed in response to external influences and societal conditioning, can obscure the radiant light of your true self. By peeling back these layers with courage and self-awareness, you can unveil the purity and authenticity that resides at the core of your being.

One of the key aspects of connecting with your spiritual essence is the practice of mindfulness and presence. Being fully present in the moment allows you to tap into the deep well of inner peace and clarity that is always available to you. By quieting the incessant chatter of the mind and tuning into the subtle rhythms of your inner world, you can access a profound sense of connection with the universal energy that flows through all of creation.

In this state of mindfulness, you may experience moments of profound insight and revelation that illuminate your path with divine guidance. These moments of clarity can serve as signposts on your journey of self-discovery, showing you the way forward with grace and purpose. Trust in the wisdom of your intuition and the gentle nudges of the universe, for they are guiding you towards a life of alignment and fulfillment.

As you deepen your connection with your spiritual essence, you may also begin to experience a heightened sense of compassion and empathy towards yourself and others. This compassionate awareness stems from the recognition that we are all interconnected and share a common source of divine energy. By embracing this interconnectedness with an open heart and a spirit of loving-kindness, you can cultivate a profound sense of unity and harmony with all beings.

Embracing your spiritual essence is a lifelong journey of self-discovery and growth, a path that invites you to explore the depths of your being with curiosity and reverence. Allow yourself to surrender to the flow of universal energy that animates your existence, trusting in the innate wisdom and guidance that is always available to you. By honoring and nurturing your spiritual essence, you can cultivate a life of purpose, joy, and fulfillment that resonates with the beauty and truth of your divine nature.

Harnessing The Power of Intention

In the vast expanse of the metaphysical landscape, the art of setting intentions emerges as a profound practice that transcends mere wishful thinking and enters the realm of conscious co-creation with the cosmic forces that govern our existence. At its core, intention-setting is a sacred act of aligning our thoughts, emotions, and actions with a specific vision or goal, thereby initiating a powerful ripple effect that reverberates throughout the fabric of reality.

Delving deeper into the essence of intention, we unravel the intricate web of interconnectedness that binds us to the energetic frequencies of the universe. By honing our focus and clarity on what we wish to manifest, we tap into the universal law of attraction, which states that like attracts like. Through this universal principle, we begin to understand the profound impact our thoughts and intentions have on the unfolding tapestry of our lives.

The practice of setting intentions goes beyond mere words or affirmations; it is a deeply transformative process that requires us to confront our innermost desires, fears, and beliefs. Through introspection and self-awareness, we unearth the hidden gems of our soul's yearnings and aspirations, illuminating the path towards our true purpose and fulfillment.

Infusing our intentions with unwavering belief and unwavering positivity acts as a potent catalyst that amplifies their vibrational resonance in the quantum field. By visualizing our desired outcomes with vivid detail and immersing ourselves in the emotions of joy, gratitude, and abundance, we signal to the universe our readiness to receive the blessings we seek.

Taking inspired action emerges as a pivotal step in the manifestation process, where we actively engage with the opportunities and synchronicities that present themselves along our journey. By aligning our thoughts, emotions, and actions towards our intentions, we establish a harmonious flow of energy that propels us towards the realization of our dreams.

Gratitude, the ultimate alchemical elixir of manifestation, serves as a potent amplifier of our intentions, magnifying their potency and accelerating their materialization. By cultivating a heart overflowing with gratitude for the blessings we already possess and the miracles unfolding in our lives, we create a powerful magnetic field that draws in abundance and prosperity with grace and ease.

In conclusion, the profound practice of intention-setting invites us to step into our role as conscious creators of our reality, where the power of our thoughts and emotions merges with the universal forces of creation to bring forth the life we envision. Through clarity, belief, inspired action, and gratitude, we unlock the expansive potential within us to co-create a reality that is in perfect alignment with our highest vision and purpose.

Healing the Wounds of the Past

In the depths of our emotional landscapes, the wounds of our past lie buried, waiting to be unearthed and healed. These wounds, often inflicted in moments of vulnerability or trauma, can shape our perceptions of ourselves, others, and the world around us. They fester beneath the surface, influencing our thoughts, beliefs, and behaviors in ways we may not even be aware of.

To embark on the journey of healing, we must first acknowledge the pain and scars we carry. It requires a willingness to confront our past experiences with courage and honesty, facing the discomfort and vulnerability that comes with delving into our emotional history. This process of introspection can be both daunting and liberating, as we unravel the layers of our past selves to reveal the core wounds that have been silently guiding us.

Self-reflection is a powerful tool in this healing process. By examining the emotional residue left by past traumas and hurts, we gain insight into the patterns and triggers that continue to shape our present reality. This heightened awareness allows us to untangle the complex web of emotions that have entwined themselves around our hearts and minds, paving the way for true healing to take place.

Forgiveness, as challenging as it may be, is essential in releasing the grip of the past on our present selves. By extending grace and compassion to those who have caused us pain, as well as to ourselves for the mistakes we have made, we free ourselves from the shackles of resentment and bitterness. Forgiveness is not an act of condoning or forgetting; rather, it is a radical act of self-love and liberation, allowing us to reclaim our power and inner peace.

Self-care and nurturing play a vital role in the healing journey. Engaging in practices that honor and nourish our physical, emotional, and spiritual well-being creates a strong foundation for healing to flourish. Whether it's through mindfulness, exercise, creative expression, or simply seeking solace in the presence of loved ones, self-care acts as a balm for the wounded soul, soothing the ache and replenishing our reservoirs of resilience.

As we navigate the winding path of healing, let us remember that it is not a linear journey with a clear endpoint. Healing is a cyclical process, ebbing and flowing like the tides of the ocean. It requires patience, self-compassion, and a willingness to embrace the discomfort of growth. With each step we take towards healing, we reclaim a piece of ourselves that was lost to the past, paving the way for a brighter and more empowered future.

Delving deeper into the realm of healing, we come to understand that the wounds of our past are not simply isolated incidents to be addressed and forgotten. They are interconnected threads woven into the fabric of our being, influencing every aspect of our lives. Our past experiences shape our beliefs, behaviors, and relationships in ways that are often subtle yet profound, creating a tapestry of emotions that color our perception of the world.

As we excavate the layers of our emotional history, we may encounter resistance and discomfort. Unearthing buried pain and confronting long-standing traumas requires courage and vulnerability, as we peel back the layers of protection we have built around our wounded selves. It is in these moments of raw exposure that true healing begins, as we shed the armor of denial and face our inner truths with honesty and compassion.

Through the process of self-reflection, we gain clarity and insight into the origins of our emotional wounds. We uncover the roots of our fears, insecurities, and self-limiting beliefs, tracing them back to the pivotal moments of our past where our inner landscape was shaped and molded. With this awareness comes the opportunity for growth and transformation, as we untangle the knots of our emotional history and create space for new patterns to emerge.

Forgiveness, a cornerstone of the healing journey, is a profound act of liberation and self-empowerment. By releasing the grip of resentment and anger towards ourselves and others, we free up energy that has been trapped in the past, allowing us to move forward with greater clarity and purpose. Forgiveness does not mean forgetting or excusing the harm that was done; rather, it is a conscious choice to let go of the pain and reclaim our sovereignty over our own emotions and well-being.

Self-care and nurturing practices serve as essential pillars of support on the healing path. Engaging in activities that replenish our energy, nourish our bodies, and calm our minds creates a sanctuary of self-love and compassion in which healing can take root and flourish. Whether it's through journaling, meditation, exercise, or spending time in nature, self-care acts as a soothing salve for the wounded soul, providing comfort and solace in moments of emotional turbulence.

In the cyclical journey of healing, we come to understand that growth is not always linear or predictable. There will be moments of regression and stagnation, where old wounds resurface and familiar patterns reassert themselves. These moments are not signs of failure but rather invitations to deepen our self-awareness and self-compassion, to tend to the wounded parts of ourselves with gentle care and patience.

As we navigate the twists and turns of the healing process, let us remember that it is a journey of self-discovery and self-empowerment. By embracing the complexities of our emotional landscape and honoring the wounds of our past, we create the fertile ground for transformation and renewal. With each step we take towards healing, we reclaim our inner light and authenticity, shining brightly as beacons of resilience and strength in a world that often seeks to dim our radiance.

Cultivating Self-Love and Acceptance

Embracing oneself fully and unconditionally is a transformative journey that requires patience, compassion, and dedication. Cultivating self-love and acceptance is a continuous practice that involves recognizing and honoring your worth, flaws, and uniqueness.

Begin by acknowledging that you are inherently deserving of love and respect, simply by virtue of being a human being. Release any harsh self-criticism or judgments you may hold against yourself, and instead, embrace a mindset of kindness and understanding.

Practice self-care rituals that nourish your mind, body, and soul. Engage in activities that bring you joy and peace, whether it's spending time in nature, reading a good book, or simply taking a moment to breathe deeply and center yourself.

Challenge negative self-talk and replace those thoughts with positive affirmations. Affirm your worthiness, strength, and beauty, both inside and out. Treat yourself with the same kindness and compassion that you would offer to a dear friend in need.

Embrace your imperfections as part of what makes you uniquely you. Recognize that no one is perfect, and it is through our flaws and struggles that we grow and learn. Allow yourself to be vulnerable and authentic, sharing your true self with the world without fear of judgment or rejection.

Forgive yourself for past mistakes and shortcomings, understanding that growth and change are inevitable parts of the human experience. Let go of any lingering guilt or shame, and instead, focus on your capacity for resilience and transformation.

By cultivating self-love and acceptance, you pave the way for a deeper connection with yourself and others. Embrace your inherent worthiness, celebrate your strengths and weaknesses, and strive to live authentically and unapologetically as the beautiful and deserving soul that you are.

Remember, self-love is not about perfection but rather about accepting yourself fully, with all your complexities and contradictions. It is about acknowledging your value as a person, regardless of external measures of success or approval from others. When you truly love and accept yourself, you radiate that love outwards, creating a positive ripple effect in your relationships and interactions with the world. So, commit to practicing self-love every day, treating yourself with kindness and compassion, and embracing your unique essence with gratitude and appreciation.

Furthermore, self-love involves setting boundaries and prioritizing your well-being. It means saying no to things that drain your energy or compromise your values, and saying yes to activities and relationships that uplift and inspire you. Self-love also encompasses self-compassion, allowing yourself to make mistakes and learn from them without berating yourself. It means treating yourself with the same level of care and understanding that you would offer to a loved one in times of need.

In addition, self-love involves cultivating a positive self-image and embracing your physical appearance with acceptance and love. Recognize that beauty comes in all shapes, sizes, and forms, and that true attractiveness radiates from within. Practice self-care routines that make you feel good and nourish your body, whether it's through exercise, skincare, or simply taking the time to relax and unwind.

Ultimately, practicing self-love is a lifelong journey that requires patience, commitment, and gentleness towards oneself. It is about recognizing your inherent worthiness and choosing to treat yourself with the same level of kindness and respect that you would offer to others. By cultivating self-love, you empower yourself to live authentically, boldly, and unapologetically, embracing all that makes you unique and deserving of love.

Igniting Your Inner Fire

In the depths of your being lies a dormant spark, patiently awaiting its moment to blaze into a radiant fire of passion and purpose. This inner fire, often overlooked or underestimated, is the driving force behind your most profound desires and aspirations. It is a primal force that sustains you in times of doubt and fuels your ambition to push beyond the limits of what you once believed possible.

To ignite this internal inferno, you must first immerse yourself in the flickering light of self-awareness. Take the time to delve deep into your innermost thoughts and feelings, uncovering the core values and passions that lie at the heart of your being. Recognize that the ignition of your inner fire requires a profound connection to your true self – a willingness to embrace your authenticity and live in alignment with your deepest desires.

As you kindle this inner flame, visualize the path ahead with clarity and intention. Envision the future you desire, painting a vivid picture of the life you wish to create for yourself. Allow this image to infuse your spirit with purpose and motivation, guiding your actions towards the manifestation of your dreams.

In the journey of igniting your inner fire, take deliberate steps towards your goals with unwavering determination. Break down your objectives into manageable tasks, each one a stepping stone towards the realization of your aspirations. Embrace the process of growth and evolution, understanding that every challenge and setback is an opportunity for learning and refinement.

Surround yourself with a tribe of kindred spirits who nurture and support your inner flame. Seek out individuals who inspire and challenge you, creating a community of like-minded souls who uplift and encourage your pursuit of greatness. Allow their energy to intertwine with your own, adding fuel to the fire that burns within you.

Remember, the ignition of your inner fire is a continual process of self-discovery and transformation. Embrace the journey with an open heart and a steadfast resolve, trusting in the power of your deepest desires to lead you towards a life of fulfillment and purpose. Let your inner fire burn brightly, illuminating your path and guiding you towards the realization of your highest potential.

Connecting With Universal Energy

In the vast expanse of the universe, beyond the realms of our physical senses, lies an unseen matrix of energy that weaves together the fabric of existence. This universal energy, sometimes referred to as chi, prana, or life force, flows through all living things, connecting us to each other and to the greater cosmic web of creation.

At its core, universal energy is pure consciousness in motion, vibrating at different frequencies to create the diverse forms and manifestations we perceive in the world. This energy is not bound by time or space but exists in a state of eternal presence, offering infinite possibilities for growth, healing, and transformation.

Through the practice of meditation, breathwork, and energy healing techniques, we can attune ourselves to the subtle nuances of universal energy and harness its power for personal and collective evolution. By quieting the mind and opening our hearts to the flow of cosmic energy, we can access higher states of awareness and align with the natural rhythms of the universe.

In Eastern philosophies such as Taoism and Yoga, universal energy is seen as the vital essence that sustains life and nourishes the soul. By cultivating a deep connection to this energy through practices like qigong, tai chi, and yoga asana, we can strengthen our vitality, balance our emotions, and harmonize our physical, mental, and spiritual bodies.

In the West, energy healing modalities such as Reiki, acupuncture, and crystal therapy work with the flow of universal energy to restore balance and harmony to the body-mind-spirit complex. These ancient healing arts recognize that imbalances in our energy field can manifest as physical or emotional ailments and seek to realign the subtle energies to promote health and well-being.

As we deepen our understanding of universal energy and its impact on our lives, we come to realize that we are co-creators of our reality, shaping our experiences through the vibrations we emit and the intentions we hold. By consciously working with universal energy, we can amplify our creative abilities, manifest our desires, and align with our soul's purpose in this lifetime.

In the grand tapestry of existence, each of us is a unique thread interwoven with the universal energy that connects us all. By honoring this connection and cultivating a mindful relationship with the cosmic forces that guide us, we can navigate the complexities of life with wisdom, grace, and compassion, knowing that we are always supported and guided by the infinite intelligence of the universe.

Embodying Authenticity in Everyday Life

Embodying authenticity goes beyond just being true to oneself; it involves a continuous process of self-discovery, self-expression, and self-compassion.

Authenticity is rooted in our ability to cultivate a deep sense of self-awareness – to understand our values, beliefs, strengths, and vulnerabilities. It requires us to reflect on our past experiences, societal conditioning, and inner conflicts to discern what truly resonates with our hearts and souls. Through this introspective journey, we unravel the layers of our authentic selves, shedding societal masks and embracing our unique essence.

As we embrace authenticity, we liberate ourselves from the confines of external validation and approval. We no longer seek validation from others but derive our sense of worth and fulfillment from within. This inner validation empowers us to make choices that align with our true selves, even if they may be unconventional or challenging.

Authenticity is also about embracing vulnerability – the willingness to show up, fully seen and heard, even when it feels uncomfortable or risky. By embracing vulnerability, we open ourselves up to deep connections with others, fostering trust, intimacy, and empathy. It is through our vulnerability that we forge genuine connections and cultivate meaningful relationships based on honesty and mutual respect.

Furthermore, embodying authenticity is an ongoing practice that requires courage and perseverance. It involves navigating moments of uncertainty, setbacks, and self-doubt with resilience and self-compassion. By honoring our authentic selves, we honor our inherent worthiness and capacity for growth, resilience, and self-love.

In essence, authenticity is not just a way of being – it is a way of living that honors our truth, integrity, and humanity. It is a path to self-discovery, connection, and liberation, inviting us to live with purpose, passion, and authenticity in every aspect of our lives. Embrace your authenticity, for it is the light that guides you towards a life of depth, meaning, and profound connection.

Nurturing Your Soul's Purpose

As you embark on the journey of nurturing your soul's purpose, it is essential to first connect deeply with your inner self and listen to the whispers of your heart. Your soul's purpose is unique to you, a divine calling that resonates with the core of your being. It is the essence of who you are and why you are here on this earth.

To nurture your soul's purpose, start by exploring what truly brings you joy and fulfillment. What lights up your spirit and makes you feel alive? Pay attention to the activities and experiences that energize you and align with your values and beliefs. These clues can lead you closer to uncovering your soul's mission.

Next, take the time to reflect on your life experiences, both the highs and the lows. Each challenge you have faced and every triumph you have celebrated has shaped you into the person you are today. Embrace these moments as valuable lessons that have guided you towards your soul's purpose.

It is also important to surround yourself with a supportive community of like-minded individuals who uplift and inspire you on your journey. Seek out mentors and role models who are living their soul's purpose authentically and learn from their wisdom and insights. Their guidance can provide valuable perspectives and help you navigate any obstacles that may arise.

As you continue to nurture your soul's purpose, remember to practice self-care and prioritize your well-being. Taking care of your physical, emotional, and spiritual health is crucial for staying aligned with your purpose and maintaining a sense of balance. Incorporate practices such as meditation, mindfulness, exercise, and creative expression into your daily routine to nurture your soul and keep your energy flowing positively.

Listen to your intuition and trust the guidance of your inner voice as you move towards living a life that is deeply fulfilling and in alignment with your true essence. Your intuition is a powerful tool that can help you navigate the twists and turns of your journey, guiding you towards opportunities that will enrich your soul and fulfill your purpose.

By nurturing your soul's purpose, you are honoring the unique gifts and talents that you bring to the world. Embrace the beauty of your authentic self and shine your light brightly, knowing that you are making a positive impact on the world around you. Live each day with intention and purpose, allowing your soul's mission to unfold in ways that surpass your wildest dreams.

Thriving in Alignment with Your True Self

As you delve deeper into the journey of self-discovery and personal growth, you come to recognize that aligning with your true self is not just a one-time endeavor but a continuous process of refinement and evolution. It requires a commitment to introspection, self-awareness, and intentional living that goes beyond surface-level actions and beliefs.

Living in alignment with your authentic essence demands a willingness to let go of outdated patterns, limiting beliefs, and societal conditioning that no longer serve your highest good. It invites you to embrace vulnerability, authenticity, and courage as you strip away the layers of false identities and masks to reveal the raw, unfiltered truth of who you are at the core.

In this state of alignment, you are not only in harmony with yourself but also with the world around you. Your energy resonates at a frequency that attracts positivity, abundance, and synchronicities, drawing towards you the people, opportunities, and experiences that support your growth and expansion.

As you navigate the twists and turns of life, staying connected to your authentic self becomes your compass, guiding you through uncertainty and adversity with unwavering clarity and resilience. It instills in you a sense of purpose, meaning, and fulfillment that transcends external circumstances and material gains, grounding you in a deep sense of inner peace and contentment.

Within the wellspring of your true self lies immense wisdom, creativity, and power waiting to be unleashed. By cultivating a deep relationship with this sacred inner essence, you tap into a source of infinite potential and possibility, allowing your unique gifts and talents to blossom and flourish in service to your highest calling and the greater good of all.

Embrace the journey of aligning with your true self as a sacred quest, a transformative odyssey that leads you back home to the truth of who you are and the beauty of your soul's purpose. Trust in the process, surrender to the flow, and allow the radiant light of your authentic essence to illuminate the path ahead as you continue to thrive in alignment with your deepest truth.

As you traverse the labyrinthine corridors of your inner landscape, you begin to unearth hidden facets of your being, each unveiling a new layer of complexity and depth to your authentic self. Through introspection and reflection, you unravel the tangled web of conditioning and expectations that have veiled your true essence, embarking on a journey of self-discovery that transcends time and space.

In the stillness of your heart, you find the whispers of your soul guiding you towards your highest truth, beckoning you to embrace the full spectrum of who you are with open arms. You come to realize that authenticity is not a destination but a way of being, a continuous dance between unveiling and integrating the different facets of your being into a harmonious whole.

With each step taken in alignment with your true self, you forge a deeper connection with the essence of your existence, tapping into a wellspring of creativity, inspiration, and intuition that flows effortlessly from the depths of your being. This inner reservoir of wisdom becomes your guiding light, illuminating the path ahead with clarity and purpose as you navigate the ebbs and flows of life with grace and resilience.

Embracing your authentic self is a revolutionary act, a radical declaration of self-love and self-acceptance that reverberates through the universe, awakening dormant potentials and possibilities within you. It is a testament to your innate worthiness and inherent divinity, a celebration of the unique expression of life that you embody in every breath and every heartbeat.

In the sacred sanctuary of your soul, you discover the infinite expanse of your being, a boundless well of love, compassion, and joy that knows no bounds. It is here, in the depths of your authenticity, that you find true liberation and liberation, a freedom that transcends the constraints of the mind and the limitations of the ego, leading you back home to the eternal truth of who you are – a radiant being of light and love, forever connected to the infinite cosmos of creation.

If it's going to be, it's up to me.
— Robert Schuller

CHAPTER 3

Setbacks Are Setups For Comebacks

Embracing Setbacks As Opportunities

When faced with setbacks in life, it can be easy to feel defeated and discouraged. It's natural to want to avoid challenges or obstacles, as they can often bring feelings of frustration and disappointment. However, what if we were to shift our perspective and see setbacks as opportunities instead? These difficult moments can serve as valuable lessons and catalysts for growth.

Setbacks are not mere roadblocks but rather pivotal moments that can shape our character and resilience. They test our resolve and determination, pushing us to go beyond our comfort zones and confront our fears. The way we choose to respond to setbacks can ultimately define our path toward success and fulfillment. Embracing setbacks as opportunities for self-improvement and personal development is a mindset shift that can lead to profound transformation.

One fundamental aspect of facing setbacks is the opportunity they provide for introspection and self-discovery. By taking the time to reflect on what went wrong and why, we can gain deeper insights into our

41

own behaviors, habits, and decision-making processes. This self-awareness is a powerful tool for growth, as it allows us to identify areas for improvement and make necessary adjustments.

Moreover, setbacks can be seen as a form of resilience training. Just as a muscle grows stronger through resistance, our emotional and mental resilience can be strengthened by overcoming challenges. Each setback we encounter presents an opportunity to build our resilience muscle, enabling us to bounce back stronger and more resilient than before.

Additionally, setbacks can also spark creativity and innovation. When faced with obstacles, we are compelled to think creatively and explore new solutions. This process of problem-solving can lead to innovative ideas and approaches that we may not have considered otherwise. By embracing setbacks as catalysts for creativity, we open ourselves up to new possibilities and ways of thinking.

In conclusion, viewing setbacks as opportunities for growth and self-improvement is essential for navigating life's challenges with grace and perseverance. By reframing setbacks as stepping stones rather than stumbling blocks, we can harness their transformative power to propel us toward greater success and fulfillment. Each setback we face is an invitation to dig deeper, rise stronger, and uncover the limitless potential within ourselves.

The Breakdown Breakthrough Principle

In the realm of human experience, the Breakdown Breakthrough Principle stands as a beacon of light in the darkest of times. It is a profound philosophy that challenges us to embrace the full spectrum of our emotions and experiences, from moments of despair and turmoil to those of triumph and clarity. At its core, this principle invites us to see breakdowns not as signs of failure, but as opportunities for growth and transformation.

When faced with a breakdown, whether it be in our personal or professional lives, we are presented with a crossroads. We can either succumb to the overwhelming weight of our challenges or rise above them with resilience and grace. The Breakdown Breakthrough Principle teaches us that the path to breakthrough is not through avoidance or denial but through confrontation and acceptance.

It is in the depths of breakdown that we are forced to confront our deepest fears and insecurities, peeling back the layers of self-deception and revealing our truest selves. This process of self-discovery is not easy, nor is it comfortable, but it is necessary for our growth and evolution as individuals. By facing our vulnerabilities head-on, we open ourselves up to a profound sense of empowerment and freedom.

As we navigate the turbulent waters of breakdown, we may find ourselves confronted with questions of identity, purpose, and meaning. We may feel lost and disoriented, unsure of where to turn or how to move forward. In these moments of darkness, it is crucial to remember that breakthrough is always within reach. It is through the process of surrender and trust that we can tap into a wellspring of creativity and resilience that guides us towards new possibilities and horizons.

The Breakdown Breakthrough Principle is a reminder that our greatest strengths often lie in our moments of weakness. It is a testament to the resilience of the human spirit and its capacity to transcend adversity and emerge stronger and more vibrant than ever before. Through the transformative power of breakdown and breakthrough, we can unlock our full potential and step into the radiant light of our true selves.

Finding Strength in Adversity

In the deepest depths of adversity, a person's character is truly put to the test. It is in these challenging moments that we are forced to confront our deepest fears, our most profound vulnerabilities, and our fundamental beliefs about ourselves and the world around us. Adversity has a way of stripping away the layers of illusion and pretense, leaving us raw and exposed to the harsh realities of life.

When faced with adversity, it is natural to feel overwhelmed, powerless, and even despairing. The weight of our struggles can seem insurmountable, the road ahead fraught with obstacles and uncertainties. Yet, it is precisely in these moments of darkness that our inner light shines the brightest. It is in the crucible of adversity that we discover the true depth of our resilience, the vastness of our courage, and the boundless potential for growth and transformation that resides within each of us.

One of the key ways to navigate through adversity is to cultivate a mindset of acceptance and surrender. Rather than resisting or fighting against our circumstances, we can choose to embrace them with an open heart and a willingness to learn and grow from the experience. By surrendering to the flow of life, we can tap into the universal wisdom that guides us through even the most tumultuous of times.

Moreover, finding strength in adversity often requires us to lean into our vulnerabilities and confront our shadows. It is through facing our deepest wounds and fears that we can begin the process of healing and transformation. By acknowledging and honoring our vulnerabilities, we not only gain a deeper understanding of ourselves but also cultivate a greater sense of compassion and empathy towards others.

In the face of adversity, it is also crucial to seek out support and connection with others. Human beings are social creatures, and we thrive in community and connection. By reaching out for help, sharing our struggles, and offering our support to others, we create a network of strength and resilience that can sustain us through even the most challenging of times.

Ultimately, the journey through adversity is a profound opportunity for growth and self-discovery. It is a chance to transcend our limitations, redefine our beliefs, and emerge stronger, wiser, and more compassion-ate than before. Adversity is not a sign of weakness but a testament to our humanity and our capacity for resilience and transformation. In the face of adversity, we have the opportunity to rise above our circum-stances and shine brightly as beacons of hope and inspiration for others on their own journey through the darkness.

Overcoming Fear and Resilience

In life, fear is a multifaceted emotion that transcends mere psychologi-cal responses and delves into the intricate workings of our subconscious mind and emotional landscape. It is a primal instinct deeply rooted in the evolutionary history of humankind, developed over millennia as a survival mechanism to protect us from potential threats and dangers. Fear serves as a powerful signal to our brains, triggering a cascade of physiological changes that prepare us to fight, flee, or freeze in the face of perceived risks.

The experience of fear is not uniform but rather unique to each individual, shaped by a complex interplay of genetic predispositions, environmental influences, past experiences, and cultural factors. Some fears may be rational, such as fear of physical harm or danger, while others may be irrational or phobia-based, stemming from subconscious anxieties and deep-seated traumas. Understanding the nuanced nature of fear requires a deep exploration of our innermost thoughts, beliefs, and experiences, as well as a recognition of the ways in which fear can manifest in our lives.

Beyond its immediate manifestations, fear can have profound im-pacts on our mental, emotional, and physical well-being. Chronic fear and anxiety can lead to a host of negative consequences, including heightened stress levels, compromised immune function, and increased risk of developing mental health disorders such as anxiety disorders or post-traumatic stress disorder (PTSD). Left unchecked, fear can become a pervasive force that limits our potential, constrains our actions, and sabotages our efforts to live authentically and fully.

The journey of building resilience in the face of fear is a transformative process that requires commitment, self-awareness, and a willingness to confront our innermost fears and uncertainties. Resilience, often described as the capacity to bounce back from adversity and thrive in challenging circumstances, is a dynamic quality that can be cultivated through intentional practices and mindset shifts. It involves developing a growth-oriented perspective that views setbacks and challenges as opportunities for learning, growth, and self-discovery.

One key component of resilience-building is the practice of mindfulness, a state of focused awareness and presence that allows us to observe our thoughts, emotions, and physical sensations without judgment. Mindfulness techniques such as meditation, deep breathing exercises, or grounding practices can help us cultivate a sense of inner calm, clarity, and resilience in the face of fear. By becoming more attuned to our inner landscape and recognizing the impermanence of our thoughts and emotions, we can develop a greater sense of emotional balance and strength to navigate through difficult circumstances.

Additionally, fostering positive relationships and seeking support from our community can be instrumental in bolstering our resilience and providing us with the emotional scaffolding needed to overcome fear and adversity. Connecting with empathetic, understanding individuals who validate our experiences and provide a safe space for us to express our fears and vulnerabilities can help us feel supported, understood, and empowered in facing our challenges.

Furthermore, practicing self-care and self-compassion is a crucial aspect of building resilience and fortifying our mental and emotional well-being in the face of fear. Engaging in activities that nourish our bodies, minds, and spirits—such as regular exercise, creative expression, time in nature, or relaxation techniques—can replenish our energy reserves and foster a sense of inner peace and equilibrium. By prioritizing our well-being and treating ourselves with kindness, patience, and acceptance, we can cultivate the resilience needed to weather life's uncertainties and difficulties with grace and strength.

In essence, overcoming fear and building resilience is a profound journey of self-discovery, growth, and transformation that requires us to delve deep into the recesses of our inner selves and confront our fears with courage and compassion. By embracing the complexity of fear, reframing negative beliefs, practicing mindfulness and self-awareness, seeking support from our community, and nurturing our well-being through self-care and self-compassion, we can unlock our inner strength and resilience to navigate through life's challenges with grace, wisdom, and resilience.

Transforming Pain Into Power

As you navigate through life's intricate tapestry of experiences, you inevitably find yourself at the crossroads of pain and adversity. These moments of profound challenge can feel like a heavy burden, weighing down your spirit and clouding your vision of the future. Yet, within the depths of suffering lies the potential for profound transformation and growth, waiting to be unearthed by those brave enough to venture into the shadows of their own soul.

When confronted with pain, it is crucial to approach it with a sense of curiosity and self-compassion. Allow yourself to sit with the discomfort, to feel its raw intensity, and to acknowledge the intricate web of emotions that accompany it. This act of radical acceptance opens the door to healing and understanding, paving the way for profound self-discovery and personal evolution.

In the alchemy of pain lies the opportunity for deep introspection and soul-searching. By delving into the roots of your suffering, you may uncover hidden patterns, unresolved wounds, or limiting beliefs that have held you captive in the realm of darkness. This courageous exploration of the self allows you to reclaim your power, to rewrite your narrative, and to transcend the constraints of your past experiences.

As you navigate the labyrinth of pain, you may find unexpected treasures hidden amidst the shadows. Strength, resilience, and a new-found sense of purpose emerge from the crucible of suffering, reshaping you into a more authentic and empowered version of yourself. Embrace these gifts with gratitude and humility, knowing that they are forged in the fires of adversity and tempered by the trials you have endured.

True growth demands that you venture beyond the confines of your comfort zone and embrace challenges as opportunities for growth and self-realization. By confronting your pain head-on, by embracing vulnerability, and by leaning into the discomfort, you unlock the transformative power within you and emerge stronger, wiser, and more whole than you ever thought possible.

In the grand tapestry of life, your journey from pain to power is a testament to the resilience of the human spirit and the boundless capacity for growth and transformation. Your story becomes a beacon of hope for those grappling with their own struggles, a reminder that even in the darkest of moments, there is always a flicker of light waiting to be kindled into a roaring flame of resilience and renewal.

Embrace the pain, honor your journey, and trust in the transformative power that lies within you. Through the crucible of suffering, you emerge not as a victim, but as a warrior of the soul, wielding the sword of self-awareness and the shield of compassion as you navigate the ever-unfolding journey of self-discovery and personal evolution.

As you continue to walk the path of self-discovery, remember that pain is not your enemy but a wise teacher guiding you towards greater self-awareness and profound growth. Each challenge that you face presents an opportunity for deep introspection and transformation, inviting you to explore the depths of your being and unearth the hidden gems of wisdom that lie dormant within you.

The journey from pain to power is not a linear path but a spiraling ascent towards a higher state of consciousness and self-realization. Embrace the twists and turns, the highs and lows, knowing that each moment of struggle is a stepping stone towards a more authentic and integrated existence. Trust in your resilience, in your capacity for growth, and in the unwavering light that shines within you, illuminating the dark corners of your soul and guiding you towards a more expansive and liberated sense of self.

In the sacred dance of pain and transformation, you are the orchestrator of your destiny, the weaver of your own tapestry, and the author of your own story. Embrace the challenges that come your way with courage and grace, knowing that within the crucible of suffering lies the infinite potential for growth, healing, and self-empowerment. Your journey from pain to power is a testament to the resilience of the human spirit and the boundless capacity for transformation that resides within you.

Turning Challenges into Triumphs

In life, we are often faced with challenges that seem insurmountable. These obstacles can come in various forms - setbacks, failures, disappointments, and hardships. However, what sets successful individuals apart is their ability to turn these challenges into opportunities for growth and triumph.

When confronted with a challenge, it's important to first acknowledge and accept the situation. Denying or avoiding the problem will only prolong the agony and prevent any progress towards a solution. By facing the challenge head-on, you can begin the process of overcoming it.

One strategy for turning challenges into triumphs is to break down the problem into smaller, manageable tasks. This not only makes the challenge seem less daunting but also allows you to make progress incrementally. Celebrate each small victory along the way, as these milestones will keep you motivated and focused on the end goal.

Another crucial aspect of overcoming challenges is maintaining a positive mindset. It's easy to get bogged down by negative thoughts and self-doubt when facing a difficult situation. However, by reframing the challenge as an opportunity for growth and learning, you can shift your perspective and approach the problem with optimism and resilience.

Seeking support from friends, family, or a mentor can also be instrumental in helping you navigate through tough times. Surround yourself with positive and encouraging individuals who believe in your potential and can provide valuable advice and guidance.

Moreover, cultivating a growth mindset is essential in transforming challenges into opportunities for personal and professional development. Embracing the belief that abilities and intelligence can be developed through dedication and hard work empowers individuals to persevere in the face of adversity. By focusing on learning and growth rather than fixed abilities, individuals are more likely to view setbacks as temporary obstacles rather than insurmountable barriers.

Furthermore, self-care and mental well-being play a vital role in overcoming challenges and achieving success. Taking care of your physical, emotional, and mental health allows you to approach challenges with clarity and strength. Engaging in activities that bring you joy, practicing mindfulness and relaxation techniques, and seeking professional help when needed are all crucial aspects of self-care that can help you navigate challenges with resilience and grace.

In essence, turning challenges into triumphs requires a holistic approach that encompasses mindset, support systems, and self-care practices. By combining these elements and approaching challenges with determination and a positive outlook, individuals can not only overcome obstacles but also emerge stronger and more resilient on the other side. Remember, challenges are not roadblocks but opportunities for growth and transformation. Embrace them with courage and confidence, and watch as you navigate through life's ups and downs with grace and resilience.

Discovering Hidden Blessings

In the depths of adversity, when all seems lost and the world feels heavy upon our shoulders, it can be easy to lose sight of the hidden blessings that lie within the darkness. The weight of our struggles can cloud our vision and make it challenging to see beyond the immediate pain and despair. However, it is in these moments of deep sorrow and hardship that the seeds of resilience and growth are often sown.

Practicing gratitude in the face of adversity is a powerful tool that can help us navigate through even the most challenging times. By focusing on the things for which we are grateful, no matter how small they may seem, we can shift our perspective and create space for hope to enter our hearts. Gratitude allows us to recognize the beauty that still exists in the world, even amid our struggles, and can serve as a guiding light to lead us out of the darkness.

Furthermore, each trial we encounter presents us with an opportunity for growth and self-discovery. Adversity has a unique way of revealing our inner resilience and strength, showing us depths of character we may never have known we possessed. Through facing our challenges head-on, we can unearth hidden reserves of courage and fortitude that empower us to overcome even the most daunting obstacles.

The true impact of hardship is often not fully realized until after the storm has passed. It is in the reflection and introspection that follows that we can begin to see the true extent of the hidden blessings that have emerged from the chaos. The lessons learned, the strength gained, and the newfound perspective on life all serve to shape us into stronger, more compassionate individuals capable of weathering any storm that may come our way.

Adversity, with its rugged exterior and harsh demeanor, often conceals within it the seeds of growth and transformation. Like a diamond forged under immense pressure, we too can emerge from our trials with a newfound inner brilliance and resilience that shines forth in the face of adversity. It is through the crucible of hardship that we are molded into our truest selves, stripped of superficial layers to reveal the core of our being, raw and unyielding.

As we navigate the storms of life, let us remember that hidden blessings can be found in even the darkest of places. They may not always be apparent at first glance, obscured by the shadows of despair and uncertainty. But with a heart open to gratitude and a spirit tempered by challenges, we can uncover the gems of wisdom and strength that lie hidden within the depths of adversity. Embrace the journey, trust in the process, and know that the hidden blessings within the darkness will guide you towards the light.

Cultivating Self-Compassion and Self-Love

In this section, we delve into the profound significance of cultivating self-compassion and self-love as fundamental pillars of resilience and personal growth. The art of self-compassion involves extending ourselves the same gentleness, warmth, and understanding that we readily offer to others in times of distress or hardship. It entails recognizing and accepting our humanness, embracing our flaws, and acknowledging that imperfection is an inherent part of the human experience.

Coupled with self-compassion, self-love is a transformative force that allows us to forge a deep, nurturing connection with ourselves. It involves honoring our intrinsic worth, celebrating our unique qualities, and fostering a profound sense of self-esteem and self-respect. By cultivating self-love, we create a foundation of unconditional acceptance that enables us to navigate life's challenges with courage, resilience, and a resilient spirit.

The practice of self-compassion and self-love demands that we challenge and reframe our inner dialogue, replacing self-criticism and judgment with self-compassionate, empowering thoughts. By offering ourselves compassion in moments of self-doubt or struggle, we cultivate a reservoir of inner strength and resilience that sustains us during difficult times. Through this compassionate self-talk, we begin to shape a narrative of self-acceptance and self-kindness that forms the bedrock of our emotional well-being.

Furthermore, engaging in acts of self-care and prioritizing our physical, emotional, and mental health are integral components of self-compassion and self-love. Setting boundaries, practicing mindfulness, and seeking support from loved ones or mental health professionals foster a nurturing environment that nurtures our resilience and fortitude. These actions not only cultivate a sense of well-being but also empower us to confront life's challenges with a renewed sense of strength and tenacity.

In essence, the journey of cultivating self-compassion and self-love is an ongoing process of self-discovery and self-affirmation. It is about embracing our vulnerabilities, honoring our uniqueness, and learning to treat ourselves with the same kindness, empathy, and understanding that we extend to others. Through the continuous practice of self-compassion and self-love, we foster a deep sense of resilience, inner peace, and unwavering self-acceptance that empowers us to navigate life's twists and turns with grace and equanimity.

Creating Your Comeback Story

In the face of adversity, it is easy to feel defeated and overwhelmed. But it is during these challenging times that we have the opportunity to create our greatest comeback story. It is in these moments that we can tap into our inner strength and resilience, and emerge stronger than ever before.

Creating your own comeback story begins with a mindset shift. Instead of seeing setbacks as obstacles, view them as opportunities for growth and transformation. Embrace the challenges that come your way, and use them as fuel to propel you forward.

One key element of creating your comeback story is to take ownership of your narrative. Reframe your experiences in a way that empowers you, rather than disempowers you. Recognize that you have the power to shape your own story, and choose to write a narrative that inspires and uplifts you.

Another important aspect of creating your comeback story is to cultivate self-compassion and self-love. Treat yourself with kindness and understanding as you navigate through difficult times. Remember that making mistakes and facing failures are a natural part of the journey, and they do not define your worth or potential.

As you work on creating your comeback story, remember to focus on the present moment. Take small steps each day towards your goals, and celebrate your progress along the way. Stay committed to your vision, even when the road ahead seems daunting.

It is essential to understand that setbacks are not a reflection of your capabilities but are stepping stones towards growth and wisdom. Embrace the discomfort and use it as an opportunity for self-reflection and improvement.

In the process of overcoming challenges, you will encounter self-doubt and fear. However, acknowledge these emotions without being consumed by them. Learn to cultivate resilience by acknowledging your fears and still moving forward with determination.

Ultimately, the essence of a compelling comeback story lies in your ability to rise above circumstances and emerge as a stronger, wiser individual. Embrace the journey, knowing that every setback is a chance for personal development and transformation. By embodying resilience, self-compassion, and a positive mindset, you can craft a narrative of triumph and resilience that inspires not only yourself but also those around you. Your comeback story is a testament to your inner strength and unwavering spirit, showcasing your capacity to turn adversity into victory.

To truly create a compelling comeback story, it's important to understand that setbacks are not failures but rather opportunities for growth. Each challenge you face is a chance to learn more about yourself, to discover your true strengths, and to cultivate resilience in the face of adversity. By embracing your setbacks as stepping stones on your journey, you can transform moments of defeat into opportunities for personal transformation and growth.

Moreover, self-compassion is a vital component of any successful comeback story. It's crucial to treat yourself with kindness and understanding, especially when facing difficult times. By practicing self-compassion, you can build a strong foundation of self-love and acceptance that will support you through the ups and downs of life.

In addition to mindset and self-compassion, having a clear vision for your comeback story is essential. Define your goals and aspirations, and stay focused on them even when faced with challenges. Remember that setbacks are temporary roadblocks that can be overcome with determination and perseverance.

As you navigate your comeback journey, don't be afraid to seek support from others. Surround yourself with a positive and encouraging community that will uplift you and help you stay committed to your goals. Remember, you are not alone in your journey, and reaching out for help is a sign of strength, not weakness.

In conclusion, creating your own compelling comeback story is a journey of self-discovery, resilience, and growth. By embracing setbacks as opportunities for learning and personal development, practicing self-compassion, staying focused on your goals, and seeking support when needed, you can transform moments of defeat into powerful stories of triumph and resilience. Your comeback story is waiting to be written – embrace the challenge, believe in yourself, and watch as you emerge stronger and more resilient than ever before.

*"Be not conformed to this world,
but be transformed
by the renewing of your mind"*
— Romans 12:2

CHAPTER 4

Change Your Mind To Change Your Life

Unleashing The Power of Your Subconscious Mind

In delving further into the intricate workings of the subconscious mind, we embark on a journey that traverses the vast expanse of our inner landscape, shedding light on the profound mysteries that shape our thoughts, beliefs, and behaviors in ways that are both fascinating and enigmatic. The subconscious mind, often likened to an iceberg, conceals the majority of its power beneath the surface, operating in the realm of the unseen and the unspoken, yet exerting a profound influence on every aspect of our conscious experience.

At the core of the subconscious mind lies a repository of memories, emotions, and experiences that have been imprinted upon our psyche since childhood, forming the tapestry of our subconscious programming. These deeply ingrained patterns and beliefs, often formed in response to past traumas or conditioning, shape our perception of reality and influence our responses to the world around us in ways that we may not fully realize.

The subconscious mind, operating outside the realm of conscious awareness, serves as a vigilant guardian of our internal landscape, filtering and interpreting the myriad stimuli that bombard our senses on a daily basis. It acts as a reservoir of stored information and emotions, serving as a wellspring of creativity, intuition, and wisdom that can guide us towards our highest potential when aligned with our conscious intentions.

Through mindful exploration and introspection, we can begin to unravel the intricate tapestry of our subconscious mind, peeling back the layers of conditioning and unconscious programming that may be holding us back from our true essence. Practices such as meditation, hypnosis, and visualization can serve as powerful tools for accessing the deeper layers of the subconscious, allowing us to reprogram outdated beliefs and patterns and realign our internal compass towards a more empowering and fulfilling direction.

By cultivating a deeper connection with our subconscious mind and integrating its wisdom into our conscious decision-making processes, we can tap into a wellspring of creativity, insight, and intuition that empowers us to navigate life's challenges with grace and resilience. Through a commitment to self-exploration and a willingness to embrace the unknown depths of our innermost selves, we can unlock the door to a world of limitless possibilities and shape our reality in ways that transcend the confines of our conscious mind.

Understanding the Impact of Childhood Beliefs

Childhood beliefs are like a silent conductor orchestrating the symphony of our lives, creating a powerful undercurrent that guides our thoughts, emotions, and actions. These beliefs are often formed in the crucible of our early experiences, etching themselves into the very fabric of our being and shaping the lens through which we view the world.

Family dynamics, with their intricate tapestry of interactions and relationships, play a fundamental role in sculpting childhood beliefs. The quality of attachment with caregivers, the dynamics between siblings, and the patterns of communication within the family unit all leave an indelible mark on a child's developing sense of self. Children learn who they are and how they fit into the world based on these relational blueprints, internalizing messages of love, worthiness, safety, or fear.

The impact of early childhood experiences extends far beyond the walls of the home, intertwining with broader societal influences to weave a complex web of beliefs. Cultural norms, societal expectations, and media messages seep into the porous minds of children, shaping their understanding of what is deemed acceptable, beautiful, or successful. These external standards can become internalized as benchmarks for self-worth, leading individuals to measure their value against external constructs rather than intrinsic qualities.

The developing brain of a child is a marvel of neuroplasticity, constantly rewiring itself in response to experiences and stimuli. The beliefs formed during these critical years become deeply ingrained in the neural circuitry, creating pathways that influence how individuals perceive themselves, relate to others, and navigate the challenges of life. These beliefs can act as either scaffolding for growth and resilience or as barriers that limit potential and hinder personal development.

Unraveling the tapestry of childhood beliefs requires a willingness to delve into the depths of the psyche, to confront the shadows of the past with courage and compassion. Through introspection, therapy, and self-inquiry, individuals can begin the journey of untangling these intricate threads, challenging ingrained beliefs, and rewriting the narrative of their lives. By reclaiming agency over their own story, individuals can cultivate a deeper sense of self-awareness, resilience, and authenticity, freeing themselves from the shackles of outdated beliefs and stepping into a new chapter of empowerment and growth.

The Creative Power of Your Thoughts

The profound intricacies of the creative power inherent within your thoughts exist as a microcosm of the universal energy that permeates the fabric of existence. Every thought that flits through the corridors of your mind carries with it the potential to shape the very essence of your reality, resonating with the cosmic symphony of creation in ways both seen and unseen.

As you navigate the labyrinth of your inner world, it is crucial to recognize the interconnected nature of your thoughts and emotions. Emotions serve as the energetic fuel that propels your thoughts into the energetic ethers of the universe, imbuing them with a resonance that reverberates far beyond the confines of your conscious awareness. Therefore, cultivating emotional intelligence and self-awareness is paramount in the endeavor to harness the full potential of your creative thoughts.

Furthermore, the power of intention acts as a guiding force that directs the trajectory of your thoughts towards manifestation. By setting clear intentions aligned with your highest truths and values, you are able to steer the course of your creative energy towards the realization of your deepest desires and aspirations. Intentionality serves as the rudder that navigates the turbulent waters of the mind, guiding your thoughts towards the shores of manifestation with unwavering precision.

Moreover, the concept of energetic alignment underscores the importance of attuning your thoughts to the frequency of your desired reality. Just as a tuning fork resonates with a specific pitch, your thoughts emit a vibrational frequency that attracts corresponding experiences into your life. By consciously aligning your thoughts with the energetic signature of abundance, love, and joy, you create a harmonious resonance that magnetizes these qualities into your reality with effortless ease.

In essence, the creative power of your thoughts transcends the boundaries of time and space, weaving a tapestry of existence that reflects the limitless potential of your innermost desires. Embrace this power with reverence and awe, for within the sacred sanctuary of your mind lies the key to unlocking a reality beyond your wildest dreams. Trust in the transformative alchemy of your thoughts, infuse them with intention and emotion, and witness as the universe conspires in your favor to bring forth the manifestations that align with your soul's highest calling.

Rewiring Your Mind For Success

Let's delve into the transformative process of rewiring your mind for success. Your thoughts have a direct impact on your reality, and by understanding how to shift your mindset, you can unlock new levels of potential and achievement.

To rewire your mind for success, it's crucial to first identify and challenge any limiting beliefs that may be holding you back. These beliefs are often deeply ingrained from past experiences or societal conditioning, but they do not define your true capabilities. By reframing these beliefs and replacing them with empowering thoughts, you can create a new mental landscape that supports your goals and aspirations.

Mindfulness and self-awareness are powerful tools in this process. By observing your thoughts and emotions without judgment, you can gain clarity on the patterns that may be hindering your success. Through consistent practice, you can train your mind to focus on positive outcomes and opportunities, rather than dwelling on past failures or self-doubt.

Visualization and affirmations are also key strategies for rewiring your mind for success. By vividly imagining yourself achieving your goals and affirming your worthiness to receive them, you can program your subconscious mind to align with your desires. This cultivates a sense of confidence and determination that propels you towards success.

Utilizing techniques such as gratitude journaling and positive self-talk can further solidify your mindset shift. By expressing thanks for the abundance in your life and speaking kindly to yourself, you reinforce a mindset of abundance and self-worth. This fosters a positive attitude that attracts more opportunities for success into your life.

As you embark on this journey of rewiring your mind for success, remember that self-compassion is key. Be gentle with yourself as you navigate the challenges of breaking free from old patterns and embracing new ways of thinking. Cultivate a mindset of growth and resilience, knowing that each step you take towards rewiring your mind is a step towards creating the life you desire.

In conclusion, rewiring your mind for success is a powerful process that can catalyze profound transformation in your life. By consistently practicing mindfulness, visualization, affirmations, gratitude, and self-compassion, you can create a mental environment that supports your goals and empowers you to achieve greatness. Trust in your journey, stay committed to your growth, and embrace the limitless possibilities that await as you reprogram your mind for success.

Breaking Free From Limiting Beliefs

As human beings, our minds are intricate and complex, shaped by a lifetime of experiences, interactions, and conditioning. Our beliefs are not isolated entities but interconnected threads that weave together the fabric of our identities. Within the realm of limiting beliefs lie deep-seated wounds, often rooted in childhood experiences or reinforced by societal expectations. These beliefs take root in our subconscious minds, subtly influencing our thoughts, emotions, and behaviors without our conscious awareness.

The process of breaking free from limiting beliefs requires a profound level of self-awareness and introspection. It necessitates a willingness to venture into the depths of our psyche, confronting the shadows that lurk beneath the surface. This journey is not for the faint of heart, as it requires us to confront our deepest fears, insecurities, and vulnerabilities. However, it is in this crucible of self-exploration that true transformation begins to take root.

One of the key mechanisms through which limiting beliefs maintain their stronghold is through the power of repetition. As we consistently reinforce these beliefs through our thoughts and actions, they become ingrained in our neural pathways, forming a seemingly impenetrable barrier to change. The first step in breaking free from this cycle is to challenge the validity of these beliefs, to question their origins, and to examine the evidence that supports or refutes them.

Another crucial aspect of dismantling limiting beliefs is to cultivate a sense of self-compassion and acceptance. Often, we internalize harsh judgments and criticisms that fuel our negative self-perceptions. By practicing self-compassion, we can begin to unravel the layers of self-doubt and self-criticism that underpin our limiting beliefs, offering ourselves the kindness and understanding we so readily extend to others.

In the process of breaking free from limiting beliefs, it is essential to cultivate a growth mindset—one that embraces challenges as opportunities for learning and growth. By reframing our perceptions of setbacks and failures as valuable learning experiences, we can shift our perspective from one of limitation to one of possibility. This mindset shift enables us to approach life with a sense of curiosity and openness, allowing us to explore new paths and possibilities previously obscured by our limiting beliefs.

Ultimately, the journey of breaking free from limiting beliefs is a deeply personal and transformative process. It requires courage, persistence, and a willingness to confront the shadows within. By embarking on this journey with an open heart and mind, we can begin to unravel the layers of conditioning that have held us back, stepping into a more authentic, empowered, and liberated version of ourselves.

Cultivating a Positive Mindset

In the quest to cultivate a positive mindset, we journey deeper into the realms of the mind, navigating the intricate pathways that shape our thoughts, emotions, and beliefs. Our mental landscape is a vast terrain, rich with the potential for growth, transformation, and resilience. At the core of this exploration lies the profound understanding that our mindset is not fixed but fluid, capable of evolving and adapting in response to our conscious intentions and subconscious programming.

Neuroplasticity, the brain's remarkable ability to reorganize and rewire itself, serves as a powerful ally in our quest for positivity. This foundational principle underscores the dynamic nature of our brains, highlighting our capacity to reshape neural connections through intentional practices and habits. By engaging in activities that stimulate neuroplasticity, such as learning new skills, challenging limiting beliefs, and practicing gratitude, we can harness the brain's innate potential for growth and change.

Positive affirmations, a cornerstone of mindset work, offer a pathway to reprogramming our subconscious mind through the repetition of empowering statements. By affirming our worth, ability, and potential, we create a fertile ground for self-belief to take root and flourish. The language we use to communicate with ourselves shapes the narrative of our lives, influencing our perceptions, behaviors, and outcomes. Through the consistent practice of positive affirmations, we can cultivate a mindset of abundance, resilience, and self-compassion that serves as a beacon of light in times of darkness.

Visualization, another potent tool in the arsenal of mindset transformation, taps into the brain's capacity to create mental images of success and achievement. By vividly imagining ourselves accomplishing our goals and dreams, we activate the brain's neural networks associated with motivation, goal-setting, and reward. This process not only fuels our motivation and determination but also primes our subconscious mind to recognize and seize opportunities for growth and success. Visualization invites us to step into the reality we wish to create, aligning our thoughts, emotions, and actions with our deepest desires and aspirations.

Mindfulness, the art of intentional presence and awareness, offers a gateway to profound inner peace, clarity, and wisdom. By cultivating mindfulness, we learn to witness our thoughts and emotions without judgment or attachment, fostering a sense of inner calm and equanimity. This practice enables us to cultivate an intimate connection with our inner world, enhancing our capacity to respond to life's challenges with grace, compassion, and resilience. Mindfulness invites us to dwell in the present moment, embracing each breath, sensation, and emotion with gentle curiosity and acceptance.

In essence, the journey towards a positive mindset is an ongoing expedition of self-discovery, growth, and transformation. By delving deep into the recesses of our minds, we uncover the hidden treasures of our true potential, resilience, and innate worth. Through the intentional cultivation of positive thinking, self-care, and mindful awareness, we open ourselves to a world of endless possibilities and growth. The path to a positive mindset is not merely a destination but a sacred journey of self-realization and empowerment, guided by the wisdom of our hearts and the resilience of our spirits.

Manifesting Your Dreams Through Belief

In a world where possibilities are endless, the key to manifesting your dreams lies in the power of belief. Belief is not just a mere thought or feeling; it is a magnetic force that can attract to you the very things you desire.

When you believe in yourself and your dreams, you are setting in motion a powerful process of manifestation. Your beliefs shape your thoughts, your thoughts shape your actions, and your actions create your reality. It all begins with a firm conviction in the potential of your dreams to become a reality.

But belief alone is not enough. You must also align your beliefs with positive thoughts and emotions. Visualize your dreams as if they have already come true, feel the joy and gratitude that comes with that realization, and let go of any doubts or fears that may stand in your way.

Trust in the process of manifestation, knowing that the universe is working in your favor to bring your dreams to life. Stay open to opportunities that come your way, take inspired action towards your goals, and have faith that everything is unfolding as it should.

Remember, your beliefs are a powerful force that can shape your reality. By holding onto a strong belief in yourself and your dreams, you are paving the way for them to come true. Trust in the power of belief, and watch as your dreams manifest before your very eyes.

As you continue on your journey of manifestation, it is important to understand the connection between your beliefs and the energy you emit into the universe. Your beliefs act as a magnet, drawing to you the people, circumstances, and opportunities that align with them. Therefore, it is vital to cultivate a mindset of abundance, positivity, and unwavering faith in the fulfillment of your dreams.

In addition to aligning your beliefs with positive thoughts and emotions, visualization can be a powerful tool in manifesting your desires. Create a clear and detailed mental image of what you wish to manifest, engaging all your senses to make the vision as vivid and real as possible. By consistently holding this vision in your mind, you are sending a powerful message to the universe about what you wish to attract into your life.

Practice gratitude for the blessings you already have and for the manifestations that are on their way to you. Gratitude amplifies the positive energy you emit, further accelerating the manifestation process. When you express gratitude for what you have and what is yet to come, you are affirming your belief in the abundance of the universe and opening yourself up to receive even more blessings.

Ultimately, the power of belief is a transformative force that can shape your reality in profound ways. By harnessing the power of belief, aligning your thoughts and emotions with your desires, and taking inspired action towards your goals, you can manifest the life of your dreams. Trust in the process, stay open to the opportunities that come your way, and have faith that the universe is conspiring in your favor. Your dreams are within reach; all you have to do is believe.

Nurturing Self-Compassion and Self-Love

In this section, we delve into the transformative power of nurturing self-compassion and self-love in our lives. These profound practices offer us a profound way to navigate the complexities of the human experience with grace and resilience.

Self-compassion is a gentle yet potent force that invites us to embrace our humanity with kindness and understanding. It is a practice of treating ourselves with the same compassion and care that we would offer to a dear friend in times of struggle or suffering. By recognizing our shared humanity and inherent imperfections, we can cultivate a deep sense of self-acceptance and inner peace. Self-compassion allows us to hold ourselves gently, acknowledging our flaws and limitations without succumbing to self-criticism or harsh judgments. It opens the door to self-empowerment and emotional well-being, guiding us towards greater emotional resilience and a more compassionate relationship with ourselves and others.

Similarly, self-love serves as a cornerstone of our well-being, inviting us to honor and celebrate our intrinsic worth. It is a practice of embracing ourselves unconditionally, recognizing and nurturing the unique qualities and strengths that make us who we are. Self-love encourages us to prioritize our own needs and cultivate a loving relationship with ourselves, fostering a deep sense of self-respect and self-appreciation. When we embody self-love, we create a nurturing environment within ourselves that allows us to flourish and grow authentically.

Embracing self-compassion and self-love requires courage and commitment. It involves stepping into a space of vulnerability and authenticity, acknowledging our vulnerabilities and insecurities with kindness and compassion. Through mindfulness practices, self-reflection, and self-care rituals, we can deepen our connection with ourselves and cultivate a profound sense of inner peace and contentment. These practices serve as powerful tools for personal growth and emotional healing, guiding us towards a life rooted in self-acceptance, resilience, and genuine happiness.

In essence, by cultivating self-compassion and self-love, we embark on a transformative journey towards self-discovery and self-fulfillment. These practices offer us a roadmap to living authentically and wholeheartedly, allowing us to embrace our true essence with grace and compassion. When we nurture self-compassion and self-love, we create a solid foundation for a life infused with meaning, purpose, and profound joy.

Embrace Change as a Gateway to Growth

Change is a fundamental aspect of life, an unavoidable force that shapes our existence in profound ways. It is the very essence of evolution, the driving force behind progress and transformation. Throughout history, societies, civilizations, and individuals have been shaped by the winds of change, adapting and evolving in response to shifting circumstances and conditions.

From a personal perspective, change can be both daunting and exhilarating. It challenges us to step out of our comfort zones, to confront our fears and uncertainties, and to embrace the unknown with open hearts and minds. It is through facing these challenges that we grow, learn, and ultimately, thrive.

At its core, change is about letting go of the past and embracing the present moment, with all its possibilities and potential. It requires us to release our attachment to what was and instead focus on what can be. It is a process of shedding old beliefs, habits, and patterns that no longer serve us, in order to make room for new experiences, opportunities, and growth.

In our modern world, where the pace of change seems to be ever accelerating, it is more important than ever to cultivate a mindset of adaptability and resilience. We must learn to ride the waves of change with grace and agility, rather than being overwhelmed by them. This requires a willingness to let go of our need for control, to embrace uncertainty, and to trust in our innate capacity to navigate the ever-shifting landscapes of life.

Change is not a linear process; it is often messy, chaotic, and unpredictable. It can bring about feelings of discomfort, anxiety, and doubt as we navigate uncharted territories and unfamiliar terrain. Yet, it is within these moments of discomfort and uncertainty that we find opportunities for growth, self-discovery, and transformation.

Embracing change requires courage, vulnerability, and a willingness to confront our deepest fears and insecurities. It asks us to be open to new possibilities, to let go of limiting beliefs, and to step into the unknown with faith and resilience. It is through this process of surrender and acceptance that we find freedom, growth, and a deeper sense of connection to ourselves and the world around us.

Change is not always easy, nor is it always welcomed with open arms. It can be disruptive, challenging, and sometimes painful. But it is through these moments of upheaval and transition that we are given the opportunity to redefine ourselves, to reevaluate our priorities, and to create new paths forward.

In the midst of change, we are forced to confront our own vulnerabilities and limitations, to let go of what no longer serves us, and to step boldly into the unknown. It is in these moments of uncertainty that we discover our true strength, our resilience, and our capacity for growth. So, let us welcome change as a gift, a catalyst for transformation, and a reminder of our inherent ability to evolve, adapt, and thrive in the face of life's ever-changing landscape.

Transforming Your Life Through Mind Mastery

In order to truly transform your life, it is essential to master your mind. Your thoughts create your reality, and by harnessing the power of your mind, you can shape a future that aligns with your deepest desires and aspirations.

Mind mastery is a journey of self-discovery and introspection, a process that requires dedication and commitment to unraveling the complexities of your inner world. It begins with cultivating self-awareness, the foundation upon which all personal growth and transformation are built. By observing your thoughts without judgment and recognizing the patterns that shape your beliefs and behaviors, you can gain valuable insights into the workings of your mind.

Self-awareness is a gateway to self-empowerment, as it allows you to take control of your thoughts and emotions rather than being swept away by them. Through mindfulness practices such as meditation, breathwork, and body awareness, you can develop a deep sense of presence and inner peace, enabling you to navigate life's challenges with clarity and grace.

Setting clear intentions is another key component of mind mastery. By defining your goals and aspirations with clarity and precision, you create a roadmap for your future and align your thoughts and actions with your highest vision. Visualizing your intentions as if they have already manifested, you send powerful signals to the universe, signaling your openness to receiving abundance and fulfillment.

Positive thinking is a cornerstone of mind mastery, as your thoughts have the power to shape your reality. By cultivating a positive mindset and focusing on the possibilities and opportunities present in every situation, you can overcome obstacles with resilience and optimism. Embracing a growth mindset, you view challenges as opportunities for learning and growth rather than insurmountable barriers.

Gratitude is a transformative practice that can deepen your sense of abundance and contentment. Taking time each day to count your blessings and express gratitude for the gifts in your life, no matter how small, opens your heart to receiving more of the good that surrounds you. Gratitude shifts your perspective from lack to abundance, fostering a mindset of appreciation and joy.

Exploring the depths of your subconscious mind is essential for uncovering hidden beliefs and patterns that may be sabotaging your success. Through practices such as hypnotherapy, journaling, and therapy, you can unearth the root causes of your limiting beliefs and reprogram your subconscious mind for success and abundance.

Embracing the concept of neuroplasticity, the brain's ability to rewire itself in response to new experiences, offers a powerful tool for cultivating a more positive and empowered mindset. By engaging in practices that promote neural plasticity, such as visualization, positive affirmations, and cognitive-behavioral techniques, you can create new pathways in your brain that support your desired outcomes.

Understanding the role of emotions in shaping your reality is crucial for mind mastery. Emotions are powerful messengers that provide valuable insights into your inner state and guide your decisions and behaviors. By developing emotional intelligence and learning to express and process your emotions in healthy ways, you can create harmony and balance in your emotional landscape.

Draw upon the wisdom of ancient spiritual practices to deepen your connection to your inner self and the universal consciousness. Practices such as mindfulness, meditation, and energy work can help you tap into a source of wisdom and guidance that transcends the limitations of the rational mind. By aligning with the universal flow and trusting in the wisdom of your intuition, you can access a wellspring of creativity and insight to support your journey of mind mastery.

By mastering your mind, you become the architect of your own reality. Take ownership of your thoughts, beliefs, and actions, knowing that you have the power to create a life of purpose, joy, and fulfillment. Trust in the infinite potential of your mind, and watch as miracles unfold in every corner of your life.

Relationships are the glue that hold our lives together.
— Coach Michael Taylor

CHAPTER 5

The Power Of Partnerships

The Magic of Vulnerability

In a world where strength and invincibility are often prized above all else, vulnerability is seen as a weakness. But in reality, vulnerability is a powerful force that can deepen connections and foster intimacy in relationships.

When we allow ourselves to be vulnerable, we open ourselves up to the possibility of true, authentic connection with others. By sharing our fears, insecurities, and uncertainties, we show a side of ourselves that is raw and real. This act of vulnerability can be terrifying, but it is also incredibly liberating.

Vulnerability paves the way for empathy and understanding. When we are able to show our true selves to others, we invite them to do the same. This mutual vulnerability creates a space of trust and openness where deeper emotional bonds can form.

Moreover, vulnerability is a catalyst for growth and self-discovery. When we allow ourselves to be vulnerable, we confront our inner demons and fears. By facing these vulnerabilities head-on, we can heal old wounds, overcome barriers, and ultimately become stronger and more resilient individuals.

In the realm of relationships, vulnerability is the key to building intimacy. It requires courage and trust to open up to another person, but the rewards are well worth it. When both partners are willing to be vulnerable with each other, they create a bond that is unbreakable and enduring.

Research has shown that vulnerability is not only essential for building strong relationships but also for personal well-being. Those who embrace vulnerability are often more resilient in the face of adversity, better able to cope with stress, and more satisfied with their lives overall. By allowing themselves to be vulnerable, individuals can experience a greater sense of authenticity and connection with others.

However, vulnerability does not come easily to everyone. It requires a willingness to let go of control, to embrace uncertainty, and to trust in the goodness of others. For some, past experiences of rejection or betrayal may make vulnerability feel like an impossible feat. In these cases, it is important to take small steps towards vulnerability, gradually building trust and opening up at a pace that feels comfortable.

Ultimately, vulnerability is a strength that should be celebrated and nurtured. It is the foundation of true connection, the pathway to personal growth, and the essence of authentic living. When we allow ourselves to be vulnerable, we open ourselves up to the beauty and the messiness of being human, and in doing so, we create a life rich in meaning and depth.

Vulnerability is not a sign of weakness but a testament to our courage and resilience. It is through vulnerability that we truly connect with others on a profound level, allowing for genuine understanding and empathy to flourish. It is a reminder that we are all imperfect beings, navigating our way through life with our fears and vulnerabilities in tow.

When we embrace vulnerability, we strip away the masks we wear and present ourselves as we truly are. This authenticity is a gift both to ourselves and to those around us, as it paves the way for genuine relationships rooted in trust and acceptance. Vulnerability allows us to be seen and understood in our entirety, creating a space for deep emotional intimacy to develop.

Furthermore, vulnerability serves as a pathway to personal growth and self-discovery. By acknowledging and facing our vulnerabilities, we confront the barriers and insecurities that hold us back. Through this process, we can heal from past wounds, overcome limiting beliefs, and emerge stronger and more resilient individuals.

In the grand tapestry of human experience, vulnerability is a thread that weaves us together in shared humanity. It is a reminder that we are all vulnerable in our own ways, and that by embracing this vulnerability, we can find strength and connection in our shared human experience. It is a reminder that vulnerability is not a weakness, but a testament to our bravery and capacity for love and connection.

Building Trust and Mutual Respect

In a world where relationships are constantly tested by distractions and conflicting priorities, building trust and mutual respect is essential for deepening connections and fostering lasting bonds. Trust is the cornerstone upon which all successful relationships are built. It is the steadfast belief in the reliability, truth, and integrity of another person. Trust allows individuals to be vulnerable, knowing that they are in safe hands and can rely on their partner to support and understand them.

To truly build trust in a relationship, consistency and transparency are key. Consistent actions and words that align with one another create a sense of predictability and reliability that is comforting to both partners. It is through repeated experiences of dependability that trust is nurtured and solidified. Trust is fragile and must be cultivated with care and consideration.

Transparency, on the other hand, involves open and honest communication, sharing thoughts, feelings, and experiences without fear of judgment. It requires vulnerability and a willingness to be authentic and genuine in expressing oneself. Transparency builds a bridge between partners, allowing for deep and meaningful connections to form. When both partners can rely on each other to be consistent and honest, a strong foundation of trust is established that can weather the storms of life.

Mutual respect goes hand in hand with trust. It is the recognition of each other's autonomy, boundaries, and individuality. Respecting your partner means valuing their opinions, beliefs, and needs, even if they differ from your own. It also involves showing appreciation for who they are as a person and acknowledging their worth and contributions to the relationship. Mutual respect creates a harmonious dynamic where both partners feel valued and understood.

Communication is a fundamental aspect of building trust and mutual respect. Open and honest dialogue creates a space for understanding and empathy to flourish. Active listening, empathy, and validation of each other's feelings are essential components of effective communication that strengthens the bonds of trust and respect. It is through clear and empathetic communication that misunderstandings are cleared, and conflicts are resolved with compassion and understanding.

Actions speak louder than words in demonstrating trust and respect. Consistently following through on promises, being there for your partner in times of need, and showing up in a reliable and supportive manner all contribute to building trust. Respecting boundaries, showing kindness, and expressing gratitude also play a crucial role in fostering mutual respect in a relationship. It is the small gestures and consistent actions that build trust over time.

As trust and mutual respect deepen, the relationship becomes a sanctuary where both partners can be their true selves without fear of judgment or rejection. This safe space allows for growth, vulnerability, and intimacy to flourish, strengthening the bond between partners even further. Trust and mutual respect create a strong foundation for a relationship to thrive and grow.

In conclusion, building trust and mutual respect takes time, effort, and dedication from both partners. By prioritizing transparency, consistency, communication, and actions that demonstrate respect and appreciation, relationships can thrive and withstand the challenges that come their way. Trust and mutual respect form the bedrock upon which all healthy and fulfilling relationships are built, forging connections that stand the test of time.

Cultivating Authentic Communication

As a writer, I believe that authentic communication is the cornerstone of meaningful human connection. It goes beyond mere words and encompasses the essence of our being - our thoughts, emotions, and intentions. Authentic communication is an art form that requires courage, vulnerability, and empathy.

Building authentic communication starts with self-awareness. By understanding our own values, beliefs, and biases, we can communicate more intentionally and align our words with our true selves. This level of self-awareness enables us to navigate through the complexities of human interaction with clarity and authenticity. It empowers us to express our thoughts and feelings honestly, without the need for pretense or façade, leading to genuine connections rooted in truth and sincerity.

Trust is another crucial element of authentic communication. It is the foundation upon which meaningful relationships are built. When trust is present, we feel safe to open up, share our vulnerabilities, and connect on a deeper level. Trust allows us to be authentic without fear of judgment or rejection, fostering an environment where communication can flow freely and authentically. This mutual trust paves the way for genuine understanding and empathy to blossom, creating a bond that transcends superficial interactions.

Active listening is a skill that is essential for authentic communication. It involves not only hearing the words being said but also understanding the emotions and intentions behind them. Through active listening, we demonstrate respect and empathy towards the speaker, showing that their words and emotions are valued and understood. This deep level of listening fosters a sense of connection and validation, enabling authentic communication to flourish and relationships to strengthen.

Non-verbal communication, such as body language and tone of voice, plays a significant role in authentic communication. Our non-verbal cues can often convey more meaning than our words, providing insight into our true emotions and intentions. Being attuned to our non-verbal cues allows us to communicate authentically, as these cues can reveal our true feelings even when our words may say otherwise. By being mindful of our non-verbal communication, we can ensure that our authentic message is accurately conveyed, leading to more meaningful and genuine interactions.

Practicing empathy is a cornerstone of authentic communication. By actively listening, understanding, and responding with compassion, we demonstrate that we genuinely care about the well-being of others. Empathy allows us to connect on a deeper level, bridging differences and fostering a sense of shared humanity. When empathy is present in communication, it creates a space for mutual understanding and support, nurturing relationships built on trust, respect, and genuine connection.

In conclusion, authentic communication is a transformative force that allows us to connect with others in a profound and meaningful way. By cultivating self-awareness, trust, active listening, non-verbal communication awareness, and empathy, we can communicate authentically, create deeper connections, and enrich our lives and those of others. Authentic communication is the bridge that connects us to one another, offering a pathway to understanding, empathy, and genuine human connection.

Nurturing Emotional Intimacy

In the realm of relationships, emotional intimacy stands as a profound and transformative force that transcends the ordinary interactions between individuals. It is the sacred space where hearts align, minds entwine, and souls connect on a level that is beyond words. This elusive yet potent essence of connection blossoms from a place of vulnerability, courage, and unwavering trust.

To truly nurture emotional intimacy is to embark on a journey of self-discovery and mutual exploration that knows no bounds. It requires a willingness to delve deep within oneself, to unearth hidden truths, fears, and desires, and to lay them bare before the other without reservations. This act of emotional exposure is not merely an exchange of words but a communion of spirits, a merging of energies that creates a profound sense of oneness and understanding.

In the sanctuary of emotional intimacy, partners find solace in the embrace of shared emotions, no matter how raw or unrefined they may be. It is a space where tears are met with compassion, anger is met with patience, and joy is met with celebration. Within this sacred container of trust, both partners feel free to express their innermost thoughts and feelings without the fear of judgment or rejection, knowing that they are accepted and cherished unconditionally.

Communication, the lifeblood of emotional intimacy, flows effortlessly and authentically between partners who are attuned to each other's needs and emotions. It is not merely about sharing words but about truly listening, with an open heart and a compassionate soul, to the unspoken messages that lie beneath the surface. It is a dance of reciprocity, where one partner's vulnerability invites the other to reciprocate in kind, creating a harmonious rhythm of mutual understanding and acceptance.

Trust, the cornerstone of emotional intimacy, is built upon a foundation of reliability, consistency, and unwavering support. It is the unspoken promise that each partner holds, a silent pact that they will stand by each other through thick and thin, through the highs and lows of life's unpredictable journey. Trust is not merely earned but nurtured, cultivated through acts of kindness, faithfulness, and steadfast presence in the face of adversity.

In the depths of emotional intimacy, love shines like a beacon, illuminating the darkest corners of the soul and bringing warmth to the coldest of hearts. It is a love that transcends the physical realm, a love that is rooted in the spiritual connection between two souls that have found their home in each other. It is a love that knows no bounds, that defies logic and reason, and that sustains and nourishes even in the face of life's greatest challenges.

Embracing emotional intimacy in your relationship is a testament to the power of vulnerability, trust, and love to transform and elevate the human experience. It is a sacred dance that requires courage, authenticity, and an open heart, but the rewards of this deep and profound connection are immeasurable. In the sanctuary of emotional intimacy, partners find not only solace and understanding but also a profound sense of belonging, acceptance, and love that transcends the ordinary and touches the divine.

The journey of emotional intimacy delves even further into the depths of the human experience, exploring the complexities of connection and the mysteries of the heart. It is a journey that unfolds like a delicate tapestry, woven with threads of shared experiences, intimate moments, and profound revelations. Each step taken in this sacred dance reveals new layers of the self, new depths of emotion, and new pathways to understanding and acceptance.

As partners navigate the intricate terrain of emotional intimacy, they discover hidden reservoirs of strength, compassion, and resilience within themselves. They learn to confront their fears, insecurities, and vulnerabilities with courage and grace, knowing that in the sanctity of their bond, they will find solace, understanding, and unwavering support. It is a journey of mutual empowerment, where each partner lifts the other up, nurtures their growth, and champions their dreams with unwavering dedication.

The dance of emotional intimacy transcends the limitations of language and logic, delving into the realm of intuitive knowing, deep empathy, and profound connection. It is a dance of the heart and soul, where words fade into the background, and emotions speak louder than any verbal expression. In this sacred space of emotional communion, partners find refuge from the storms of life, a safe harbor where they can weather any challenge with strength, resilience, and unwavering love.

The bond forged through emotional intimacy becomes a source of endless inspiration, a wellspring of creativity, and a foundation for growth and transformation. It is a deep well of connection that nourishes the soul, fuels the spirit, and enlivens the senses with a profound sense of purpose and meaning. It is a journey that leads partners to the very core of their being, where they discover the true essence of themselves and each other, shining like brilliant stars in the vast expanse of the universe.

In the tapestry of emotional intimacy, partners find not only solace and understanding but also a profound sense of meaning, belonging, and fulfillment. It is a sacred dance that transcends the ordinary and touches the divine, a journey that leads partners on a path of self-discovery, mutual exploration, and spiritual growth. Through the power of vulnerability, trust, and love, emotional intimacy becomes a guiding light, illuminating the darkness, dispelling fear, and revealing the boundless beauty of the human heart.

The Dance of Give and Take

In the intricate tapestry of relationships, the dance of give and take transcends mere actions; it embodies the very essence of human connection. It is a dance of vulnerability and strength, of selflessness and self-awareness, weaving a bond that is both resilient and tender.

Giving in a relationship is an art of the heart, a manifestation of love and care that flows freely and generously. It is the act of offering support, kindness, and understanding without reservation or expectation. When we give from the depths of our being, we create a sacred space where compassion and empathy nourish the roots of our connection, allowing it to flourish and thrive.

Yet, in this dance of give, there is also the profound act of receiving, of allowing oneself to be vulnerable and open to the love and support of another. Taking in a relationship is not a sign of weakness, but rather a testament to our humanity; it is an acknowledgment of our interdependence and a willingness to be seen and accepted as we are.

The balance of give and take in a relationship is a delicate equilibrium that requires mindfulness, communication, and mutual respect. It is about honoring one's own needs and boundaries while also being attuned to the needs of our partner, creating a dynamic of reciprocity and harmony that sustains the ebb and flow of love and understanding.

In moments of challenge and conflict, when the dance falters and the steps grow uncertain, it is essential to engage in honest and compassionate communication. This is the foundation upon which trust is built, allowing the dance of give and take to evolve and deepen, forging a bond that is resilient in the face of adversity.

The dance of give and take is not just a series of actions but a reflection of the complex interplay of emotions, desires, and vulnerabilities that define the human experience. When we give without expectation and receive with gratitude and openness, we create a reciprocal exchange that nurtures the soul and strengthens the bond between two individuals.

At the heart of this dance lies empathy, the ability to truly understand and connect with the feelings and experiences of our partner. By listening deeply, offering support without judgment, and being present in both joyful and challenging moments, we build a foundation of trust and intimacy that sustains us through life's ups and downs.

Ultimately, the dance of give and take is a sacred ritual that weaves the threads of intimacy and connection, creating a tapestry of love and understanding that binds two souls together in a harmonious symphony of shared experiences and mutual growth.

Creating Shared Goals and Dreams

In addition to setting shared goals and dreams, it is crucial for partners in a relationship to cultivate a deep sense of empathy and understanding towards each other. Empathy involves the ability to truly comprehend and resonate with your partner's emotions, perspectives, and experiences.

When partners practice empathy, they create a safe and nurturing space where both individuals feel heard, valued, and supported. This profound level of understanding fosters a sense of emotional intimacy and closeness, strengthening the bond between partners.

Empathy is not merely about feeling sympathy for your partner's emotions; it goes beyond that to involve actively listening, validating their feelings, and seeking to understand their point of view. By demonstrating empathy, partners show that they care deeply about each other and are willing to make the effort to connect on a deeper level.

Moreover, empathy can help partners navigate conflicts and challenges that may arise in their relationship. When disagreements occur, approaching them with empathy can lead to more constructive and effective communication, as both partners aim to understand each other's perspectives and find common ground.

Practicing empathy in a relationship also builds a sense of trust and mutual respect. When partners consistently show empathy towards each other, they demonstrate their commitment to the relationship and create a strong foundation of emotional support and understanding.

When partners truly understand and empathize with each other, they are better equipped to validate each other's emotions and communicate their needs effectively. This level of emotional intelligence and connection allows couples to navigate the complexities of life together with grace and understanding.

Furthermore, empathy in a relationship can lead to a deeper sense of intimacy and satisfaction. By empathizing with their partner's feelings and experiences, individuals show that they are invested in their partner's well-being and happiness, creating a sense of emotional closeness that can strengthen their bond over time.

In essence, empathy is the foundation upon which healthy and fulfilling relationships are built. By prioritizing empathy and understanding in their relationship, partners can forge a deep and meaningful connection that stands the test of time, weathering any challenges that come their way with love, compassion, and mutual respect.

Overcoming Challenges Together

In times of adversity, the strength of a relationship is truly put to the test. Challenges can arise unexpectedly, shaking the very foundation of our connection and leaving us feeling vulnerable and unsure. It is during these moments that we must come together as a united front, facing the obstacles head-on with resilience and determination.

Communication is key when navigating difficulties together. Open and honest dialogue allows both partners to express their concerns, fears, and frustrations in a safe environment. By actively listening to one another and offering support and understanding, couples can find common ground and work towards a solution together.

It is important to remember that challenges are a natural part of any relationship and should be viewed as opportunities for growth and strengthening bonds. Instead of turning against each other in times of crisis, partners should strive to face the obstacle as a team, drawing upon each other's strengths and fostering a sense of unity.

Building resilience as a couple involves staying connected, even in the face of adversity. This can be achieved through acts of kindness, gestures of love, and unwavering support for one another. By standing together through the storms of life, couples can emerge stronger and more connected than ever before.

Moreover, during challenging times, it is imperative to prioritize self-care and individual well-being. Each partner should take the time to address their own needs and emotions, allowing for personal growth and self-reflection. By maintaining a strong sense of self, individuals can contribute positively to the relationship and support their partner more effectively.

Furthermore, seeking professional guidance or therapy can be beneficial in navigating challenging times as a couple. A trained therapist can provide tools and strategies for effective communication, conflict resolution, and building resilience together. Seeking outside help is not a sign of weakness but rather a proactive step towards strengthening the relationship.

In conclusion, overcoming adversity as a couple requires patience, understanding, and a commitment to working together towards a common goal. By facing challenges head-on, communicating openly, and prioritizing individual and collective well-being, couples can emerge from difficult times stronger, more connected, and ready to face whatever comes their way.

Adversity can reveal hidden strengths within a relationship that were previously untapped. Through facing and overcoming challenges together, couples can develop a deeper understanding of each other's capabilities and resilience. The shared experience of navigating adversity can create a bond that is forged through fire, solidifying the foundation of the relationship and creating a sense of trust and mutual respect.

It is important to recognize that everyone copes with adversity differently, and it is essential to approach challenging situations with empathy and compassion towards one another. Couples must respect each other's coping mechanisms and provide support in a way that aligns with their partner's needs. By demonstrating understanding and patience during tough times, couples can build a stronger connection and foster a sense of teamwork in overcoming obstacles.

Moreover, maintaining a sense of perspective during adversity can help couples navigate challenges with a clearer mindset. By reminding themselves of the bigger picture and focusing on long-term goals and values, partners can find the strength to persevere through difficult times. This shared vision can serve as a guiding light, reminding couples of what truly matters and providing a sense of purpose during turbulent times.

In times of adversity, it is essential for couples to practice self-care individually and collectively. Taking the time to prioritize mental, emotional, and physical well-being can help partners recharge and stay resilient in the face of challenges. Encouraging each other to engage in self-care activities, such as exercise, meditation, or hobbies, can promote a sense of balance and rejuvenation within the relationship.

Lastly, overcoming adversity as a couple requires a willingness to learn and grow from the experience. Reflecting on the challenges faced, identifying areas for improvement, and committing to ongoing communication and collaboration can help couples emerge stronger and more connected. By viewing adversity as an opportunity for personal and relational growth, couples can navigate challenges with grace and resilience, ultimately deepening their bond and fortifying their relationship for the future.

Celebrating Successes and Milestones

In times of triumph, it is essential to revel in the joy and celebrate the victories that come our way. Celebrating successes and milestones is not just about recognizing achievements; it is about acknowledging the hard work, dedication, and perseverance that led to those moments of triumph.

As we mark these milestones, it is important to take the time to reflect on the journey that brought us to this point. Remember the challenges we overcame, the setbacks we faced, and the lessons we learned along the way. It is through these struggles that we gain the strength and resilience to push forward and reach our goals.

Sharing these moments of success with others is equally important. Celebrating with loved ones, friends, and colleagues not only amplifies the joy but also strengthens the bonds that connect us. It is a reminder that we are not alone in our journey and that our achievements are shared victories that enrich all of our lives.

Furthermore, celebrating successes and milestones serves as motivation for future endeavors. It instills a sense of confidence and belief in our abilities, encouraging us to aim higher and strive for even greater achievements. By recognizing and celebrating our successes, we can fuel our ambition and drive to continue pushing ourselves toward our dreams.

In the grand scheme of life, it is these moments of celebration that bring color and vibrancy to our journey. They remind us of the beauty of progress, the sweetness of triumph, and the joy of shared accomplishments. So, as we raise a toast to our successes and milestones, let us savor the moment and cherish the memories that will forever be etched in our hearts.

These moments of triumph also serve as beacons of hope and inspiration for those around us. Our successes can motivate others to pursue their dreams and persevere in the face of adversity. By sharing our triumphant moments, we create a ripple effect of positivity and encouragement that can uplift and inspire those in our circle and beyond.

Moreover, celebrating our achievements allows us to practice gratitude and cultivate a mindset of abundance. It encourages us to appreciate the journey, not just the destination, and to be thankful for the opportunities and experiences that have shaped us along the way. This attitude of gratitude not only enhances our sense of fulfillment but also attracts more blessings and abundance into our lives.

As we bask in the glow of our triumphs, let us also remember the importance of humility. Acknowledging our achievements with grace and humility keeps us grounded and reminds us that success is not a solitary journey. It is the result of teamwork, support, and collaboration with others who have contributed to our growth and development.

In essence, celebrating our successes and milestones is a multifaceted endeavor that goes beyond mere revelry. It is a profound acknowledgment of our journey, a source of inspiration for others, a practice of gratitude, and a display of humility. So, let us continue to celebrate our victories with joy and gratitude, knowing that each triumph is a testament to our resilience, determination, and unwavering spirit.

Sustaining Lifelong Partnerships

In the exploration of Sustaining Lifelong Partnerships, delving deeper reveals the intricate dynamics at play in fostering a strong and enduring bond between two individuals. Beyond the surface level of communication, trust, and respect, lies a rich tapestry of emotions, experiences, and shared growth that shape the foundation of a lifelong partnership.

Communication is not merely about speaking and listening; it is about truly understanding and empathizing with your partner's thoughts, feelings, and perspectives. It involves active listening, genuine curiosity, and the ability to communicate both joy and sorrow openly and authentically. Effective communication encompasses verbal and non-verbal cues, allowing partners to connect on a deeper level and establish a secure framework for expressing emotions, resolving conflicts, and sharing intimate moments.

Trust is the cornerstone upon which a lifelong partnership is built. It requires vulnerability, consistency, and the willingness to be transparent and honest with each other, even in times of uncertainty or conflict. Trust is not easily won but is essential for creating a safe and secure space where both partners can express themselves freely without fear of judgment or betrayal. Building trust involves demonstrating reliability, integrity, and empathy in all interactions, fostering a sense of emotional security and mutual understanding that forms the core of a resilient and enduring partnership.

Mutual respect goes beyond mere courtesy; it is about valuing and honoring each other's individuality, boundaries, and aspirations. It involves recognizing and celebrating the unique qualities and contributions that each partner brings to the relationship, while also fostering a sense of equality and partnership in decision-making and goal-set-ting. Respecting each other's differences and appreciating the strengths and weaknesses that make each partner unique enhances the depth and richness of the partnership, creating a sense of harmony and acceptance that strengthens the bond between two individuals.

Emotional intimacy is the deep connection that stems from shared experiences, vulnerability, and a sense of being truly seen and under-stood by your partner. It requires ongoing nurturing through gestures of affection, quality time spent together, and expressions of love and appreciation that reinforce the emotional bond between partners. Cultivating emotional intimacy involves creating a safe and supportive environment where both partners can express themselves authentically, share their innermost thoughts and feelings, and engage in meaningful conversations that deepen their connection and foster a sense of close-ness and intimacy.

Shared goals and dreams act as a compass guiding the couple through life's ups and downs, providing a sense of purpose, direction, and unity. By aligning their visions for the future and working towards common objectives, partners can cultivate a sense of team spirit and mutual support that strengthens their bond and deepens their con-nection. Setting goals together, whether they be personal, professional, or relational, fosters a sense of collaboration, motivation, and shared achievement that strengthens the partnership and reinforces the sense of unity and togetherness between partners.

In facing challenges together, partners learn to rely on each other for support, wisdom, and encouragement. By weathering storms as a united front and overcoming obstacles hand-in-hand, couples forge a resilience that fortifies their relationship and reaffirms their commit-ment to each other. Overcoming challenges strengthens the bond be-tween partners, fostering a sense of trust, unity, and shared strength that enables couples to navigate the complexities of life with grace, resilience, and unwavering dedication to each other.

Celebrating successes and milestones, no matter how big or small, serves as a reminder of the shared journey that partners have embarked upon together. By recognizing and cherishing moments of achievement, growth, and joy, couples can cultivate a sense of gratitude and appreciation for the blessings in their lives and the strength of their partnership. Celebrating milestones, accomplishments, and special occasions together not only reinforces the sense of togetherness and connection between partners but also creates lasting memories and shared experiences that enrich the fabric of their relationship and deepen their bond over time.

In essence, sustaining a lifelong partnership requires a deep and abiding commitment to nurturing the love, trust, respect, intimacy, shared goals, resilience, and celebration that form the bedrock of a thriving and enduring relationship. It is a journey of self-discovery, mutual growth, and unwavering dedication that enriches the lives of both partners and creates a tapestry of love that endures the test of time. Nurturing these essential elements of a lifelong partnership ensures a strong and enduring bond that continues to evolve and flourish over the years, fostering a deep sense of connection, support, and love that sustains partners through life's myriad challenges and joys.

You are the average of the five people you hang out with the most.
— Jim Rohn

CHAPTER 6

Your Vibe Attracts Your Tribe

The Power Of Your Vibe

As a writer, I understand the profound impact of our energy and aura on our interactions and experiences. Our vibe is like a silent language that speaks volumes, transcending words and reaching straight to the core of who we are. It is the essence of our being, the invisible thread that connects us to the world around us.

The energy we emit is a reflection of our inner landscape - a reflection of our thoughts, emotions, beliefs, and desires. It is a subtle language that communicates our essence to others, drawing in those who resonate with our frequency and repelling those whose energies do not align with ours. When we are in tune with our true selves and radiate positive vibes, we create a magnetic field that attracts abundance, opportunities, and meaningful connections into our lives.

Our vibe is not just a surface level projection; it is a deep reflection of our inner state of being. It is the accumulation of our experiences, our traumas, our joys, and our sorrows - all woven into the fabric of our existence. When we take the time to cultivate self-awareness, practice self-love, and align with our purpose, we elevate our vibration and create a ripple effect that reverberates out into the world.

By tuning into our vibe and consciously shaping our energy, we become co-creators of our reality. We attract experiences and relationships that mirror our inner state, guiding us towards growth, expansion, and fulfillment. When we embrace the power of our vibe and harness it for our highest good, we unlock a world of infinite possibilities and potentialities.

Our vibrational frequency is constantly in flux, influenced by our thoughts, beliefs, and the environments we inhabit. When we are mindful of the energy we are emitting, we can intentionally shift our vibration to align with our highest intentions and goals. This practice of energetic alignment allows us to tap into the universal flow of abundance and manifest our desires with greater ease and grace.

When we are in harmony with our true essence and radiate our authentic vibration, we emit a resonance that reverberates throughout the cosmos. This energetic signature acts as a beacon, guiding us towards experiences, opportunities, and connections that are in alignment with our soul's journey. Trust in the power of your vibe, for it is a sacred language that speaks directly to the universe, co-creating a reality that is in perfect harmony with your highest self.

Understanding Your Tribe

Understanding your tribe on a deeper level requires a multifaceted approach that goes beyond surface-level interactions and observations. As a famous writer, you have a unique opportunity to delve into the complexities and nuances of human relationships and group dynamics, offering valuable insights that can enrich your storytelling and resonate with your readers.

One aspect to consider is the role of shared values and beliefs within your tribe. By exploring the underlying principles and philosophies that unite your community, you can uncover the common threads that bind individuals together and shape their collective identity. Whether it's a commitment to creativity, innovation, social justice, or personal growth, understanding the shared values of your tribe can provide a foundation for meaningful collaboration and cohesion.

Additionally, it is important to recognize the impact of history and shared experiences on the formation of your tribe. Past successes, challenges, and milestones can shape the group's identity and sense of purpose, influencing their relationships and interactions in the present. By acknowledging and honoring the unique journey that has brought your tribe together, you can deepen their connection and foster a sense of continuity and belonging that transcends individual differences.

Furthermore, exploring the diversity and complexity of your tribe can offer valuable insights into the unique strengths and perspectives that each member brings to the table. Embracing the richness of human diversity within your community can spark creativity, innovation, and resilience, as individuals with varied backgrounds and experiences come together to tackle challenges and pursue shared goals. Encouraging inclusivity and celebrating the unique contributions of each member can foster a sense of appreciation and empowerment that strengthens the fabric of your tribe.

Ultimately, understanding your tribe is an ongoing process of exploration, reflection, and growth. By embracing the multifaceted nature of human relationships and group dynamics, you can nurture a culture of empathy, collaboration, and mutual respect that sustains and enriches your community over time. Through your insights and storytelling prowess, you have the power to illuminate the depth and complexity of human connection, inspiring others to build meaningful relationships and communities based on trust, understanding, and shared values.

Embracing Authentic Connections

In a world brimming with fleeting connections and superficial interactions, the essence of authentic human connection becomes increasingly vital yet elusive. The digital age, though fostering connectivity in unprecedented ways, often serves as a veil that obscures the raw, unfiltered depths of genuine relationships. As we glide through the virtual realm, a barrage of likes, shares, and comments can deceive us into believing that we are fostering meaningful connections when, in reality, we may be standing on the surface, peering into a shallow pool of curated images and curated selves.

Authentic connections, however, transcend the superficiality and demand a courageous plunge into vulnerability and truth. They require a willingness to strip away the polished facades we so meticulously construct and reveal the raw, unvarnished essence of our being. It is in these moments of unfettered authenticity that true intimacy blossoms, forging bonds that weather the storms of life and resonate with a profound resonance that echoes through the corridors of our souls.

The tapestry of authentic connections weaves its intricate threads through the spectrum of human relationships - from the tender kinship of friends who see us through our darkest hours to the fiery passion of lovers who ignite our hearts with their unwavering presence. In the realm of professional partnerships, authentic connections pave the way for collaboration rooted in mutual respect, honesty, and a shared commitment to excellence.

Navigating the labyrinth of modern existence, it is easy to succumb to the allure of shallow interactions and fleeting connections that offer the illusion of social currency without demanding emotional investment. Yet, it is in the embrace of authenticity that we unearth the true treasures of human connection - the solace of being truly seen and accepted, the catharsis of sharing our unfiltered truths, and the ecstasy of basking in the unfiltered light of genuine love and understanding.

In a world awash with noise and distractions, the silent language of authenticity beckons us to listen, to speak, and to connect with a depth and sincerity that transcends the constraints of time and space. As we navigate the ebb and flow of relationships in this ever-evolving landscape, let us remember that the true currency of connection lies not in the number of likes we receive but in the depth of love and understanding we give and receive in return. May we honor the sacred art of authentic connection, for it is in the sharing of our genuine selves that we discover the boundless beauty of human connection.

Finding Your Tribe In A Digital Age

In today's fast-paced digital age, it can be challenging to find and connect with like-minded individuals who resonate with our values and beliefs. However, with the power of technology and social media, we have a unique opportunity to expand our tribe beyond physical boundaries and geographical limitations.

The digital landscape offers a plethora of platforms and online communities where we can discover and interact with people who share our interests and passions. Whether it's joining a Facebook group dedicated to a specific hobby, participating in online forums and discussions, or connecting with like-minded individuals through Instagram, Twitter, or LinkedIn, the internet provides a virtual space for us to find our tribe.

It's essential to approach online connections with authenticity and mindfulness. While digital platforms offer a convenient way to meet new people, it's crucial to prioritize quality over quantity when building your online tribe. Seek out individuals who uplift and inspire you, who challenge you to grow and evolve, and who share similar values and goals.

When engaging with your digital tribe, remember to be respectful and considerate of others' perspectives and boundaries. Foster meaningful relationships by actively participating in conversations, offering support and encouragement, and contributing valuable insights and knowledge.

Additionally, don't underestimate the power of face-to-face interactions. While online connections are valuable, nothing can replace the depth and intimacy of in-person relationships. Consider organizing meetups, events, or gatherings to bring your digital tribe together in the physical world and strengthen your bonds.

In the digital age, finding your tribe is no longer limited by physical proximity. Embrace the opportunities that technology offers to connect with like-minded individuals, share your passions, and build a supportive community that enriches your life.

Furthermore, when navigating the vast expanse of the digital realm, it's important to remain discerning and selective about the communities you choose to engage with. Not every online space will be conducive to building genuine connections or fostering meaningful relationships. Take the time to explore different platforms, observe the dynamics within various groups, and seek out environments that align with your values and interests.

As you traverse the virtual landscape in search of your tribe, remember that authenticity is key. Be true to yourself, share your unique perspectives and experiences, and allow your genuine self to shine through in your interactions with others. Building a digital tribe based on authenticity and mutual respect will cultivate a sense of belonging and support that transcends online boundaries and resonates on a deeper level.

In the interconnected world of the internet, our tribe can span continents and time zones, bringing together individuals from diverse backgrounds and experiences. Embrace the richness and diversity of your digital community, celebrate the unique contributions of each member, and foster connections that empower and uplift all involved.

Above all, remember that the strength of your tribe lies in the quality of the relationships you cultivate. Nurture connections with intention, invest time and energy in building trust and understanding, and create a supportive network that enriches your life and empowers you to grow and thrive in the digital landscape.

Celebrating Diversity With Your Tribe

In a world filled with diverse cultures, backgrounds, and beliefs, celebrating diversity within your tribe is essential for fostering a strong and inclusive community. Embracing the unique perspectives and experiences that each member brings to the table can lead to a rich tapestry of ideas and connections that can enhance the overall dynamic of your tribe.

Diversity is not just about differences in ethnicity or race; it also encompasses variations in gender, age, sexual orientation, socio-economic status, abilities, and more. Each individual's identity is a complex blend of multiple factors, and recognizing and honoring this complexity is fundamental to creating a truly inclusive environment.

One powerful way to celebrate diversity within your tribe is by actively seeking out and amplifying marginalized voices. This includes making space for individuals who may have historically been underrepresented or marginalized within your community. By elevating these voices and centering their experiences, you can work towards a more equitable and inclusive tribe where all members feel valued and heard.

In addition to listening to and learning from one another's stories, it's important to also take action to address systemic inequalities and injustices that may exist within your tribe or the broader society. This could involve implementing policies and practices that promote equity and inclusion, as well as challenging discriminatory behaviors or attitudes when they arise. By committing to ongoing education and advocacy, you can work towards creating a more just and equitable community for all.

Creating a culture of belonging within your tribe is another key aspect of celebrating diversity. This involves fostering a sense of connection and community among members, where everyone feels welcomed and supported for who they are. By organizing inclusive events, offering opportunities for collaboration and connection, and providing resources for personal development, you can cultivate a sense of unity and belonging that transcends individual differences.

Furthermore, celebrating diversity within your tribe is not just a one-time effort but an ongoing commitment to growth and evolution. It requires a willingness to engage in uncomfortable conversations, confront biases and prejudices, and continually strive to create a more inclusive and equitable community for all. By embracing diversity as a source of strength and resilience, you can build a tribe that is not only diverse but also united in its shared commitment to justice, understanding, and compassion.

In conclusion, celebrating diversity within your tribe is a transformative journey that requires intention, reflection, and action. By embracing the richness of individual differences and creating a culture of belonging and inclusion, you can cultivate a vibrant and resilient community that thrives on the unique contributions of its members. Let diversity be your guiding light towards a more just, equitable, and harmonious tribe where every voice is heard, valued, and uplifted.

The Art of Giving and Receiving Support

In a world where individualism often reigns supreme, it can be easy to forget the power of giving and receiving support within our tribes. The art of supporting one another is a vital component of building strong and lasting connections. It is a give-and-take dynamic that fosters trust, intimacy, and mutual growth.

Support can come in many forms - a listening ear, a helping hand, a word of encouragement. It requires empathy, compassion, and a willingness to be vulnerable. When we support others, we create a safe space for them to express themselves without judgment or fear. We offer our strength as a foundation for their growth and development.

Equally important is the ability to receive support graciously. Allowing others to help us can be a humbling experience, but it is essential for our own well-being. By accepting support, we affirm our interconnectedness and acknowledge that we cannot navigate life's challenges alone. It opens the door for deeper bonds to form within our tribe and reinforces the notion that we are in this together.

The art of giving and receiving support is a reciprocal relationship that requires balance and trust. It is a continual exchange of energy that strengthens the fabric of our tribe and ensures that no one is left behind. When we embrace this art with an open heart and mind, we create a community that thrives on mutual care and empowerment.

In this interconnected web of support, there lies a profound understanding of our shared humanity. We recognize that each member of our tribe brings their own unique strengths and struggles, and by coming together in solidarity, we can uplift and empower one another. Through acts of kindness and compassion, we not only enrich the lives of those around us but also cultivate a sense of belonging and purpose within ourselves.

The ripple effect of supporting one another extends far beyond our immediate circle. It spreads out into the world, inspiring others to create their own communities of care and connection. When we lead by example and offer our support freely, we sow the seeds of kindness and empathy that have the power to transform lives and societies. It is in these moments of shared humanity that we discover the true potential of our collective strength and resilience.

As we navigate the winding paths of life, let us remember the art of giving and receiving support. Let us embrace the vulnerability it entails and the profound connections it cultivates. Together, we can create a world where compassion and solidarity thrive, where no one is left to face their struggles alone.

Overcoming Obstacles Together

As our tribe navigates the treacherous terrain of life's challenges, we are reminded of the profound impact of unity in times of adversity. The essence of overcoming obstacles together lies not only in pooling our individual strengths and resources but also in cultivating a shared sense of purpose and resilience that transcends the trials we face.

In the intricate tapestry of human connection, we find solace and strength in the bonds we create with our tribe members. These bonds are not merely superficial ties but rather deep-rooted connections that anchor us in times of turmoil. Through mutual support and understanding, we find a sense of belonging and security that enables us to confront even the most daunting obstacles with unwavering determination.

In the face of adversity, communication emerges as a vital tool in our arsenal, enabling us to navigate the complexities of our challenges with clarity and purpose. By fostering a culture of open dialogue and active listening within our tribe, we create a platform for sharing experiences, perspectives, and innovative solutions that empower us to surmount obstacles collectively.

Furthermore, the act of overcoming obstacles together serves as a transformative catalyst for personal growth and self-discovery. It is through the crucible of challenges that we unearth hidden reservoirs of strength, courage, and resilience that propel us towards our fullest potential. As we confront setbacks and setbacks with our tribe by our side, we not only fortify our resolve but also cultivate a deep-seated sense of empowerment and solidarity that sustains us through the darkest of times.

In essence, the journey of overcoming obstacles together with our tribe transcends mere survival; it signifies a profound evolution of spirit and character. Through shared experiences, mutual support, and unwavering solidarity, we forge a bond that transcends individuality and enriches the collective tapestry of our tribe. Embrace the transformative power of unity within your tribe, and together, you can conquer any obstacle that stands in your path, emboldened by the unshakeable resolve and interconnectedness of those who walk alongside you.

Manifesting Your Best Life With Your Tribe

In the intricate tapestry of life, the power of manifesting one's best life with the unwavering support of a trusted tribe resonates at the deepest levels of human connection and potential. The synergy that arises when individuals come together to uplift, inspire, and elevate each other holds the key to unlocking profound transformations and achieving unprecedented heights of personal fulfillment.

Central to the manifestation process within a tribe is the art of setting intentions and goals with unwavering clarity and conviction. By articulating one's deepest desires and aspirations to the universe and sharing them openly with the tribe, an individual not only declares their intentions but also invites the collective energy and support of like-minded souls. This act of vulnerability and transparency not only strengthens one's resolve but also creates a powerful web of accountability and encouragement within the tribe.

Moreover, the visualization of success and the cultivation of positive energy within the tribe serve as pillars of manifestation that elevate the entire process to sublime realms of possibility. As tribe members collectively focus their thoughts, emotions, and intentions on the shared vision of a best life lived, the resonance of their collective energy reverberates across the universe, aligning the forces of creation to bring their desires into tangible reality. Through the practice of visualizing success and basking in the radiant positivity of the tribe, individuals can infuse their manifestation journey with an unwavering sense of purpose, alignment, and divine grace.

Gratitude, as a cornerstone of the manifestation process within a tribe, holds the power to deepen the bonds of connection, appreciation, and abundance among its members. By cultivating a mindset of gratitude and acknowledging the invaluable support, love, and positivity that the tribe offers, individuals not only attract more blessings and opportunities into their lives but also strengthen the fabric of their collective manifestation journey. The act of expressing heartfelt gratitude towards the tribe members and the universe for the abundance and blessings that flow into their lives enriches the manifestation process with a sense of humility, grace, and profound interconnectedness.

Furthermore, the act of surrendering to the flow of life and trusting in the divine timing of the universe can amplify the manifestation process within a tribe. When individuals release their attachment to specific outcomes and surrender to the greater wisdom and intelligence of the cosmos, they create space for miracles, synchronicities, and unexpected blessings to unfold in their lives. Trusting in the unfolding of their highest good and remaining open to the infinite possibilities that lie beyond their limited perceptions can catalyze the manifestation of their deepest desires with grace, ease, and abundance.

The power of community in the manifestation journey cannot be underestimated, for it is within the supportive embrace of a tribe that individuals can find solace, inspiration, and unwavering encouragement to pursue their dreams with zeal and determination. By surrounding themselves with individuals who mirror their highest potential, share their vision of a best life lived, and hold space for their growth and evolution, individuals can transcend their limitations, expand their horizons, and step into the fullness of their being with courage, resilience, and authenticity.

Ultimately, the journey of manifesting one's best life within a tribe is a sacred dance of co-creation, where the energies of intention, visualization, gratitude, surrender, and community converge to orchestrate a symphony of transformation, growth, and fulfillment. As individuals align themselves with the highest vibrations of love, abundance, and harmony within the tribe, they not only elevate their personal manifestation journey but also contribute to the greater tapestry of universal evolution, awakening, and expansion. Through the conscious cultivation of intentions, visualizations, gratitude, surrender, and community support, individuals can navigate the labyrinth of life with grace, purpose, and divine guidance, anchoring their dreams into reality and infusing their existence with beauty, wonder, and limitless possibilities.

"What is hope but a feeling of optimism, a thought that says things will improve, it won't always be bleak, there's a way to rise above the present circumstances. Hope is an internal awareness that you do not have to suffer forever and that somehow, somewhere there is a remedy for despair that you will come upon if you can only maintain this expectancy in your heart."

– Wayne W. Dyer

CHAPTER 7

The Power Of Optimism

Embracing the Bright Side

In a world filled with challenges and uncertainties, it can be easy to get bogged down by negativity and despair. But amidst the chaos and darkness, there is always a glimmer of light waiting to be embraced. Embracing the bright side is not just a fleeting moment of positivity; it is a profound shift in perspective that can transform our entire outlook on life.

When we consciously choose to see the good in every situation, no matter how challenging it may be, we open ourselves up to a world of possibilities and opportunities. It is in these moments of embracing the bright side that we discover our inner strength, resilience, and capacity for growth.

Embracing the bright side is a practice that goes beyond mere optimism; it is a deep-seated belief in the innate goodness of the world and the human spirit. By cultivating gratitude, positive affirmations, and staying mindful of our thoughts and emotions, we can train our minds to see the beauty in every moment, no matter how small or fleeting.

As we journey through life, it is important to remember that embracing the bright side is not about denying the darkness or pretending that everything is perfect. Rather, it is about acknowledging the challenges we face while choosing to focus on the light that guides us through those challenges.

In the depths of our struggles, it is easy to lose sight of the positive aspects of life. Yet, it is precisely in these challenging moments that embracing the bright side becomes even more critical. It is a beacon of hope that can guide us through the darkest of times, reminding us that there is always a glimmer of light, no matter how faint it may seem.

To truly embrace the bright side is to cultivate a mindset of resilience and optimism, even in the face of adversity. It is about finding gratitude in the small moments, practicing kindness towards ourselves and others, and choosing to see the beauty in the world around us.

So, as you navigate the ebb and flow of life's ups and downs, remember to embrace the bright side with an open heart and a courageous spirit. Look for the light in the darkness, the joy in the sorrow, and the hope in despair. In doing so, you will discover a world filled with love, laughter, and endless possibilities.

The Magic of Positivity

In a world where darkness often threatens to overshadow the light, the power of positivity stands as a beacon of hope, guiding us through tumultuous times and inspiring us to see beyond the shadows. The magic of positivity does not simply lie in its ability to elevate our mood or brighten our day; it runs much deeper, permeating the very fabric of our existence and shaping the course of our lives in ways we may not even realize.

At its core, positivity is a mindset, a way of viewing the world through a lens of hope, gratitude, and resilience. It is a conscious decision to focus on the good in every situation, to choose optimism over pessimism, and to cultivate a sense of inner peace and contentment that transcends external circumstances.

When we choose to adopt a positive outlook, we are not denying the challenges and obstacles that lie before us; rather, we are choosing to approach them with courage and optimism, believing in our ability to overcome them and emerge stronger on the other side. Positivity empowers us to confront adversity with grace and determination, knowing that every setback is an opportunity for growth and every hardship is a stepping stone towards personal evolution.

But the magic of positivity goes beyond mere mindset – it is a force that aligns us with the abundant flow of the universe, opening doors and paving the way for miracles to unfold. When we radiate positivity, we become beacons of light in a world that can often feel dark and overwhelming, drawing towards us the energy of abundance, prosperity, and joy.

Studies have shown that a positive mindset can have profound effects on our physical health as well. By reducing stress levels, boosting our immune system, and promoting overall well-being, positivity not only nurtures our mental and emotional health but also strengthens our bodies, making us more resilient in the face of illness and disease.

Furthermore, positivity has the remarkable ability to attract success and fulfillment into our lives. When we maintain a positive attitude and align ourselves with the vibration of joy and gratitude, we broadcast a powerful signal to the universe that we are ready to receive all the good that life has to offer. Opportunities align, connections are made, and dreams begin to manifest with surprising ease, all because of the transformative power of positivity.

In essence, positivity is not just a fleeting emotion or a passing fancy; it is a way of living, a philosophy that invites us to embrace the limitless possibilities that exist within and around us. It is a reminder that in a world filled with challenges and uncertainties, the magic of positivity is a beacon of hope, a guiding light that leads us towards a life of abundance, joy, and profound fulfillment.

Finding Joy in Everyday Moments

In a world that often feels chaotic and overwhelming, it can be easy to overlook the simple joys that surround us every day. Yet, if we take the time to pause and truly appreciate the beauty in the ordinary, we can find a sense of peace and contentment that transcends the challenges of our daily lives.

Finding joy in everyday moments starts with a shift in perspective. Instead of focusing on what is lacking or going wrong, we can choose to direct our attention to the small moments of beauty and delight that are always present if we only open our eyes to them. Whether it's the warmth of the sun on our skin, the sound of a bird singing outside our window, or the laughter of a loved one, there are countless opportunities to find joy in the mundane.

Practicing mindfulness is a powerful tool for cultivating a deeper appreciation of the present moment. By slowing down and immersing ourselves fully in our surroundings, we can savor the richness of each experience and connect more deeply with the world around us. Mindfulness allows us to notice the intricate details that we may have previously overlooked – the play of light and shadow, the gentle rustling of leaves in the wind, or the subtle shades of color in a flower petal. These small, seemingly insignificant moments can hold immense beauty and wonder if we are willing to pay attention.

Gratitude also plays a crucial role in uncovering joy in everyday moments. When we take the time to acknowledge and express gratitude for the blessings in our lives, no matter how small, we shift our focus from scarcity to abundance. Gratitude opens our hearts to the countless gifts that surround us – the supportive relationships, the moments of connection, the opportunities for growth and learning. By cultivating a mindset of gratitude, we train ourselves to see the beauty and goodness that surrounds us, even in the most challenging circumstances.

Moreover, the practice of seeking joy in everyday moments can have profound effects on our well-being. Research has shown that individuals who consistently engage in activities that bring them joy, no matter how small, experience higher levels of happiness, resilience, and overall satisfaction with life. By making a conscious effort to notice and appreciate the beauty and wonder in our daily lives, we create a positive feedback loop that enhances our mental and emotional well-being.

Ultimately, finding joy in everyday moments is a practice that requires intention and commitment. It's about choosing to see the light in the darkness, the beauty in the chaos, and the joy in the mundane. By cultivating a mindset of mindfulness and gratitude, we can uncover a sense of joy that is ever-present, waiting to be discovered in each and every moment of our lives.

Nurturing a Hopeful Heart

In a world where uncertainty seems to permeate every aspect of our lives, where the future feels shrouded in shadows of doubt and fear, cultivating a hopeful heart becomes not just a choice but a necessity. It is a beacon of light in the darkness, a compass guiding us through the stormy seas of life, a warm embrace in the coldest of nights.

Hope is not a mere fleeting emotion; it is a steadfast belief that transcends mere optimism. It is the unwavering conviction that, no matter how tough the road may be, there is always a flicker of light at the end of the tunnel. It is the resilience to rise from the ashes of despair, the courage to face adversity head-on, and the faith that better days are not just a distant dream but a tangible reality waiting to be embraced.

Nurturing a hopeful heart requires tending to the garden of your soul with care and intention. It involves taking the time to nourish your spirit with moments of joy, connection, and peace. It means surrounding yourself with positivity, seeking out sources of inspiration, and sowing seeds of gratitude and love in the fertile soil of your heart.

Self-compassion plays a crucial role in nurturing hope. By treating yourself with kindness and understanding, by forgiving your mistakes and celebrating your victories, you create a safe harbor within yourself where hope can thrive. This inner sanctuary becomes a wellspring of strength and resilience, a sanctuary where the flame of hope burns bright even in the darkest of times.

Maintaining a hopeful heart also involves embracing uncertainty with open arms. Life is a journey filled with twists and turns, surprises and challenges, but by letting go of the need for control and learning to trust in the unfolding of our path, we can navigate the unknown with grace and poise. It is in these moments of surrender that hope shines the brightest, guiding us towards new horizons and unseen possibilities.

As we continue to walk the winding road of life, let us remember the power of a hopeful heart. Let us nurture it with compassion, fortify it with resilience, and allow it to light the way towards a brighter, more fulfilling future. For in the depths of our being, hope is not just a fleeting emotion but a powerful force that has the potential to transform our lives and the world around us.

Hope is the spark that ignites our dreams, the fuel that propels us forward, and the anchor that keeps us grounded in times of turmoil. It is a beacon of light in the darkest of nights, a whisper of encouragement in moments of doubt, and a steady hand to guide us through the labyrinth of life's challenges.

In the tapestry of human experience, hope weaves a golden thread that connects us all, reminding us of our shared humanity and our capacity for resilience and renewal. It is the silent prayer in the hearts of those who refuse to give up, the rallying cry of the oppressed and downtrodden, and the rallying cry of the oppressed and downtrodden, and the enduring legacy of those who have dared to dream against all odds.

So, let us hold fast to hope, even when the storms of life rage around us. Let us cultivate it like a precious flower, tending to it with care and attention, so that its fragrance may uplift not only our own spirits but also those around us. For in the face of adversity, in the presence of uncertainty, in the midst of darkness, hope is our constant companion, our guiding light, and our greatest ally on the journey of life.

The Transformative Power of Gratitude

Gratitude is a profound force that has the potential to shape our lives in ways we may not fully comprehend. It is a practice that transcends cultural and religious boundaries, deeply rooted in the human experience. When we cultivate gratitude, we open ourselves up to a world of abundance and possibility, where even the smallest moments can hold immense meaning.

Studies have shown that individuals who regularly practice gratitude experience a wide range of physical and mental health benefits. From reduced stress levels to improved sleep quality, the act of acknowledging and appreciating the good in our lives has a profound impact on our overall well-being. Gratitude has even been linked to lower blood pressure, stronger immune function, and a greater sense of vitality.

Beyond its effects on our health, gratitude also plays a critical role in our relationships with others. When we express appreciation for the people in our lives, we not only strengthen our bonds with them but also foster a sense of trust and mutual respect. Gratitude has the power to deepen connections, bridge divides, and nurture a sense of community and belonging that is essential to our emotional well-being.

In times of difficulty and uncertainty, cultivating a practice of gratitude can act as a beacon of light in the darkness. By focusing on the blessings and joys that exist even amidst pain and struggle, we can find moments of solace and hope that help us navigate life's challenges with resilience and grace. Gratitude allows us to shift our perspective, to see beyond immediate hardships and setbacks, and to find strength in the knowledge that there is always something to be thankful for.

Incorporating gratitude into our daily lives can take many forms – from a simple thank-you to a heartfelt reflection on the beauty of the natural world. By making space for gratitude, we invite more love, joy, and abundance into our lives, creating a ripple effect that touches not only ourselves but all those around us. Gratitude is a practice that reminds us of the richness and beauty of life, urging us to open our hearts and minds to the boundless possibilities that await when we approach the world with a spirit of thankfulness and appreciation.

Through the lens of gratitude, we can also cultivate a deeper sense of mindfulness and presence in our daily lives. When we take the time to truly appreciate the beauty and wonder of the world around us, we become more attuned to the richness of each moment, finding joy and meaning in even the simplest of experiences. Gratitude encourages us to slow down, to pause and reflect on the countless gifts that surround us each day – from the warmth of a smile to the colors of a sunset.

Moreover, practicing gratitude can help us navigate the inevitable challenges and obstacles that life presents with resilience and fortitude. By shifting our focus towards the positive aspects of our lives, we can build a foundation of strength and optimism that supports us in times of difficulty. Gratitude allows us to reframe our experiences, to find silver linings in the darkest clouds, and to discover the seeds of growth and transformation hidden within adversity.

In essence, gratitude is a practice that holds the power to transform our lives from the inside out. By cultivating a spirit of appreciation and thankfulness, we open ourselves up to a world of abundance, connection, and possibility. Gratitude is not merely a fleeting emotion but a way of being, a way of seeing the world with eyes of wonder and a heart filled with appreciation. In embracing gratitude, we embrace life itself – in all its complexity, beauty, and profound mystery.

Overcoming Adversity with Optimism

In the face of adversity, it can be easy to feel overwhelmed and defeated. Challenges and obstacles may arise that threaten to knock us off course and shake our confidence. However, it is during these difficult times that our true strength and resilience are put to the test.

Optimism plays a crucial role in overcoming adversity. It is the unwavering belief that even in the darkest of moments, there is light at the end of the tunnel. Optimism enables us to see possibilities where others see roadblocks and to maintain a positive outlook despite the challenges we face.

When faced with adversity, it is important to acknowledge our emotions and allow ourselves to feel them fully. However, it is equally important not to dwell on negativity or let it consume us. Instead, we must focus on shifting our perspective and finding the silver lining in every situation.

One powerful way to overcome adversity with optimism is to practice self-reflection and gratitude. By taking the time to reflect on past challenges we have overcome and the lessons we have learned, we can gain a sense of perspective and resilience. Additionally, expressing gratitude for the blessings in our lives, no matter how small, can help shift our focus from what is lacking to what is abundant.

Furthermore, seeking support from loved ones and surrounding ourselves with a positive and encouraging community can help bolster our optimism during tough times. Connecting with others who uplift and inspire us can provide much-needed encouragement and strength to persevere through adversity.

Ultimately, overcoming adversity with optimism is a choice that we make every day. It is a mindset that empowers us to face challenges head-on, believing in our ability to overcome them and emerge stronger on the other side. By cultivating a sense of optimism and resilience, we can navigate life's ups and downs with grace and courage, knowing that brighter days lie ahead.

In today's fast-paced world, where challenges seem to multiply by the day, maintaining a positive outlook can seem like an uphill battle. However, the power of optimism lies in its ability to transform obstacles into opportunities for growth and development.

One key aspect of practicing optimism in the face of adversity is to engage in positive self-talk. By reframing negative thoughts and focusing on constructive and empowering language, we can shift our mindset from one of defeat to one of resilience. Additionally, setting realistic goals and celebrating small victories along the way can help bolster our optimism and motivation.

Another crucial aspect of overcoming adversity with optimism is to cultivate a sense of mindfulness and presence. By staying grounded in the present moment and avoiding getting caught up in worries about the future or regrets about the past, we can better navigate the challenges that come our way with clarity and composure.

Moreover, acknowledging our own agency and taking proactive steps to address the challenges we face can help empower us and instill a sense of control amidst chaos. By focusing on solutions rather than dwelling on problems, we can harness our inner strength and resilience to tackle adversity head-on.

In conclusion, while adversity may be an inevitable part of life, our response to it is within our control. By embracing optimism as a guiding principle and cultivating a mindset of resilience and gratitude, we can not only weather the storms that come our way but emerge from them stronger and more resilient than ever before.

Spreading Sunshine Through Kindness

In a world that can often feel dark and challenging, there is a powerful antidote that has the ability to bring light and warmth to even the coldest of hearts: kindness. The simple act of spreading sunshine through acts of kindness can have a ripple effect that touches the lives of countless others.

Kindness is not just a gesture; it is a mindset, a way of being in the world that seeks to uplift and inspire. It is a beacon of hope in a world that can sometimes feel bleak. When we choose to approach each interaction with a spirit of kindness, we are not only brightening someone else's day, but we are also enriching our own souls.

Kindness has a profound impact not only on the receiver but also on the giver. Studies have shown that acts of kindness can boost mood, increase feelings of satisfaction, and even improve physical health. When we extend kindness to others, we are also benefiting ourselves in ways we may not even realize.

One of the beautiful things about kindness is that it knows no bounds. It doesn't matter how big or small the act is; what matters is the intention behind it. A kind word, a thoughtful gesture, a helping hand – these are the building blocks of a more compassionate world.

When we make a conscious effort to spread sunshine through kindness, we not only make a positive impact on those around us, but we also contribute to a collective energy of goodness and light. Kindness is contagious, and the more we practice it, the more it spreads to others.

But beyond the immediate effects of kindness, there is a deeper layer to its impact. Kindness connects us to our shared humanity, reminding us that we are all interconnected in this vast tapestry of existence. It reminds us that despite our differences, we all crave love, understanding, and acceptance.

Kindness also has the power to break down barriers and build bridges between individuals and communities. It transcends language, culture, and background, creating a common ground where understanding and empathy can flourish. In a world that is often divided by walls of misunderstanding and prejudice, kindness has the potential to be a unifying force that brings us closer together.

Moreover, kindness is not just a fleeting moment of goodness; it is a practice that can be cultivated and nurtured over time. By making a conscious effort to prioritize kindness in our daily lives, we can create a ripple effect that radiates outwards, touching the lives of those we may never even meet.

In the end, kindness is a gift that we give not only to others but also to ourselves. It is a reminder of our capacity to bring light and warmth into the world, even in the face of darkness. So let us all be bearers of this precious gift, spreading sunshine through acts of kindness and creating a brighter, more compassionate world for all.

Radiating Positivity in a Negative World

In a world that often feels consumed by darkness and negativity, the importance of radiating positivity cannot be overstated. As we navigate the complexities of life, we encounter a myriad of challenges and obstacles that can easily dim our spirits and cloud our perspectives. It is during these turbulent times that our ability to cultivate and share positivity becomes even more crucial.

Positivity is not merely a fleeting emotion or shallow disposition; it is a profound mindset and way of being that can have a transformative impact on both ourselves and those around us. By choosing to focus on the good amidst the bad, we tap into a wellspring of resilience, hope, and inner strength that allows us to navigate even the most trying circumstances with grace and optimism.

Self-care and self-love are foundational pillars in the practice of radiating positivity. When we prioritize our well-being and nurture our minds, bodies, and spirits, we not only replenish our own energy but also cultivate a reservoir of positivity that can be shared with others. By tending to our own needs and finding joy and fulfillment within ourselves, we become beacons of light, illuminating the path for those who may be struggling in the darkness.

Empathy and kindness are powerful tools in the arsenal of those who seek to radiate positivity in a negative world. By extending compassion and understanding to others, we not only uplift their spirits but also create a ripple effect of goodwill that can reverberate far beyond our immediate interactions. Small acts of kindness, whether a listening ear, a helping hand, or a simple gesture of appreciation, can serve as potent catalysts for positive change and connection in a world that is often fragmented and divided.

Choosing to embody positivity and optimism in the face of adversity is a courageous act of defiance against the prevailing narratives of despair and cynicism. By looking for the silver linings, finding moments of joy and gratitude, and sharing our light with others, we become agents of transformation and ambassadors of hope in a world that is in desperate need of both. When we commit to radiating positivity, we not only uplift ourselves and those around us but also contribute to the collective effort of making the world a brighter, more hopeful place for all beings.

At its core, the practice of radiating positivity is about embracing the full spectrum of human experience and recognizing that even in the darkest of times, there is always a glimmer of light waiting to be discovered. It is a conscious choice to focus on the beauty, the resilience, and the potential for growth that exists within every challenge and setback. By shifting our perspectives and approaching life with a mindset of abundance and gratitude, we not only empower ourselves to overcome obstacles but also inspire others to see the world through a lens of possibility and hope.

In a society that often glorifies cynicism and pessimism, choosing to radiate positivity can feel like a radical act of rebellion. It requires us to challenge our own conditioning and societal norms, to resist the pull of negativity and despair, and to dare to believe in the innate goodness and potential for change that resides within each of us. It is a constant practice of mindfulness, self-awareness, and intentional action that requires us to be vigilant in our thoughts, words, and deeds.

As we journey through life, facing its myriad challenges and triumphs, let us remember the power and impact of radiating positivity. Let us be beacons of light in a world that is often shrouded in darkness, shining our love, compassion, and hope brightly for all to see. For it is through our collective efforts to cultivate positivity and spread kindness that we can truly make a difference and create a more beautiful, harmonious world for ourselves and future generations.

"What I know for sure is that you feel real joy in direct proportion to how connected you are to living your truth."
— Oprah Winfrey

CHAPTER 8

Find Your Truth

The Divine Thread That Unites Us All

In the intricate tapestry of life, the divine thread that unites us all weaves through the very essence of our existence, connecting every soul in a symphony of oneness. This sacred, invisible bond transcends the limitations of time and space, guiding us towards a deeper understanding of our interconnectedness with all beings.

At the core of this divine thread lies the transformative power of love, a force so profound that it has the ability to heal, uplift, and unite humanity in ways beyond comprehension. Love is the universal language that speaks to the depths of our souls, reminding us of our shared divinity and intrinsic worth. It is through love that we come to recognize the beauty in diversity, honoring the unique journeys and experiences that shape each individual.

When we embrace this divine thread of love and unity, we open ourselves to a profound sense of empathy and compassion towards others. We acknowledge the inherent dignity and sacredness within every being, fostering a deep sense of connection that transcends superficial differences and biases. Through acts of kindness, understanding, and acceptance, we create a ripple effect of positive energy that reverberates throughout the collective consciousness.

As we continue to honor and nurture this divine thread that binds us together, we awaken to the truth of our interconnectedness with all of creation. We come to realize that we are not separate entities existing in isolation, but integral parts of a larger whole. Through this awareness, we cultivate a sense of belonging and unity that transcends borders, cultures, and ideologies, fostering a shared sense of purpose and harmony.

In celebrating the beauty of our shared humanity and embracing the divine thread that unites us all, we sow the seeds of a more compassionate, empathetic, and inclusive world. By recognizing the sacredness within each individual we encounter, we embody the essence of love and oneness that is at the heart of our existence. As we continue to weave this divine thread into the fabric of our lives, we co-create a reality filled with peace, understanding, and a deep sense of interconnectedness that transcends all barriers.

This interconnectedness extends beyond the physical realm and into the realm of the spiritual. We are not just connected through our shared experiences and emotions, but also through our spiritual essence. Each soul is a sacred spark of the divine, interconnected with all other souls in a cosmic dance of energy and light.

When we tap into this spiritual interconnectedness, we awaken to a deeper sense of purpose and meaning in our lives. We realize that we are here to not only journey through our individual paths but to also contribute to the collective evolution of consciousness. By honoring this spiritual thread that connects us all, we align ourselves with the higher vibrations of love, wisdom, and compassion that flow through the universe.

In this deep interconnectedness, we find solace in the understanding that we are never truly alone. Our souls are intertwined with countless others, creating a vast web of energy that transcends time and space. As we open ourselves to this profound connection, we expand our awareness beyond the limitations of the ego and embrace the universal truth of our oneness with all of creation.

Embracing this expanded vision of interconnectedness, we step into a higher state of being where love and unity are not just ideals to strive towards, but the very essence of our existence. In every interaction, every thought, and every breath, we have the opportunity to honor the divine thread that unites us all, weaving a tapestry of compassion, understanding, and unity that resonates throughout the cosmos.

Embracing Personal Spiritual Exploration

Personal spiritual exploration is a journey of self-discovery that unfolds like a series of intricate tapestries woven from the threads of our thoughts, emotions, and experiences. It is a profound and transformative process that invites us to peel back the layers of conditioning and societal expectations to uncover the essence of our existence.

At its core, personal spiritual exploration is a quest for meaning, purpose, and connection. It is a journey that beckons us to look beyond the surface of our daily lives and delve into the mysteries of the universe. Through practices such as meditation, prayer, contemplation, and introspection, we begin to unravel the intricate web of our inner landscape, revealing hidden truths and insights that guide us on our path.

This journey of self-discovery is not without its challenges and obstacles. It can be a tumultuous and unpredictable voyage, filled with moments of doubt, confusion, and inner turmoil. Yet, it is through these struggles that we find our strength and resilience, forging a deeper connection to our innermost selves and the greater cosmic tapestry of existence.

As we traverse the landscapes of personal spiritual exploration, we may encounter a multitude of spiritual teachings, traditions, and practices that offer guidance and illumination along the way. Each insight, revelation, and epiphany serves as a stepping stone on our journey, deepening our understanding of the divine mysteries that underpin our reality.

Ultimately, personal spiritual exploration is a sacred dance between the self and the cosmos, a journey of awakening and transformation that leads us to a profound sense of purpose, fulfillment, and interconnectedness with all life. It is a journey that transcends time and space, weaving together the threads of our individual experiences into the rich tapestry of universal consciousness.

Breaking Free From the Constraints of Religious Dogma

Religious dogma, while providing comfort and structure, can also limit one's spiritual growth by imposing rigid boundaries and stifling personal exploration. Breaking free from these constraints involves a courageous journey of self-discovery, where individuals must unravel the threads of indoctrination and conditioning that have bound them to external beliefs and practices. This process requires deep introspection, critical thinking, and a willingness to confront the uncomfortable truths that lie beneath the surface of our consciousness.

As individuals embark on this journey of spiritual liberation, they may encounter resistance from within themselves and from external sources that seek to maintain the status quo. The path to freedom from religious dogma is not easy, as it requires individuals to face their deepest fears, doubts, and insecurities in order to transcend the illusions that have shaped their worldview. It is a process of shedding layers of false identities and unveiling the authentic self that lies at the core of their being.

Breaking free from religious dogma is not merely a rejection of external beliefs but a profound reclamation of one's inner truth and sovereignty. It is a journey towards self-empowerment, where individuals reclaim their innate sense of agency and authority over their spiritual path. Through this process, individuals liberate themselves from the confines of external authority and awaken to the boundless potential that resides within them.

As individuals navigate the complexities of breaking free from religious dogma, they may experience moments of profound transformation, epiphany, and awakening. It is through these moments of revelation that individuals glimpse the vastness of their spiritual potential and the interconnectedness of all existence. By embracing the unknown and surrendering to the mysteries of the universe, individuals open themselves to a more expansive and inclusive vision of spirituality that transcends the limitations of dogmatic belief systems.

In the end, the journey of breaking free from religious dogma is a sacred odyssey of self-discovery, transformation, and integration. It is a journey of liberation that leads individuals towards a deeper understanding of themselves, their place in the world, and their connection to the divine. Through courage, wisdom, and love, individuals can transcend the constraints of religious dogma and embrace a more profound and illuminated vision of spirituality that honors the complexity and diversity of human experience.

Unveiling the Power of Connection and Oneness

In our exploration of the profound concept of connection and oneness, we are invited to dive even deeper into the intricacies of this universal truth. At the core of our being, beyond the illusions of separateness and individual identity, lies a profound interconnection that weaves together the fabric of existence.

This interconnectedness is not limited to the physical realm but extends into the realms of energy, consciousness, and spirit. It is a reminder that at the most fundamental level, we are all expressions of the same divine essence, interconnected and united in our shared journey through life.

When we embrace the understanding of oneness, we start to see the world through the eyes of unity and harmony. We realize that each being, each element, and each experience is a vital thread in the tapestry of creation, contributing to the intricate dance of existence. This awareness brings a sense of reverence for the interconnected web of life and the sacredness of all beings.

Through the practice of mindfulness and introspection, we can deepen our connection to the oneness that permeates all of existence. By quieting the chatter of the mind and tuning into the subtler frequencies of awareness, we can tap into the universal consciousness that unites us all. In this space of profound unity, we transcend the limitations of the ego and open ourselves to the limitless possibilities of interconnectedness.

As we awaken to the oneness that underlies all creation, we also become attuned to the rhythms and cycles of nature. We recognize that we are not separate from the Earth and all its inhabitants but intrinsically linked to the intricate ecosystems that sustain life. This realization fosters a sense of responsibility and stewardship for the planet, inspiring us to live in harmony with nature and honor the interconnected web of life.

Moreover, the understanding of oneness invites us to expand our sense of empathy and compassion towards all beings. When we recognize the divinity within ourselves and others, we cultivate a deep sense of interconnected empathy that transcends boundaries of race, religion, and culture. This compassion becomes a guiding light, illuminating the path towards greater understanding and unity among humanity.

In this tapestry of interconnectedness and oneness, we find a profound sense of purpose and meaning. We realize that our individual actions ripple out into the world, shaping the collective reality in which we live. By aligning ourselves with the principles of unity, love, and compassion, we can co-create a world where harmony, peace, and abundance are the guiding forces.

May this exploration of oneness and interconnectedness inspire us to live in harmony with all beings and honor the sacred bond that unites us in the infinite tapestry of existence.

Discovering the Universal Truths Across Religions

In the exploration of universal truths within diverse religious traditions, one cannot ignore the profound concept of transcendence. Transcendence refers to the idea that there exists a reality beyond our ordinary human experience, a realm of existence that is beyond the limitations of time, space, and material form. This idea of transcending the physical world is central to many spiritual paths, from the Christian belief in the transcendent nature of God to the Hindu concept of attaining moksha, liberation from the cycle of birth and death.

Moreover, the notion of impermanence is another universal truth that reverberates through various religious teachings. Impermanence emphasizes the transient nature of all things in the material world, reminding us of the inevitability of change and the impermanence of our physical existence. From the Buddhist teaching of anicca to the Taoist understanding of the ever-changing flow of the Tao, the recognition of impermanence invites us to embrace the present moment with gratitude and mindfulness, knowing that all things are fleeting.

Furthermore, the concept of unity or oneness is a central theme that runs through many spiritual traditions. This idea of unity speaks to the interconnectedness of all beings and the underlying unity of existence itself. Whether it is the Advaita Vedanta teaching of non-duality, the Native American concept of the interconnected web of life, or the mystical experiences of unity found in Sufism, the recognition of oneness invites us to transcend boundaries and divisions, seeing beyond the illusions of separateness to the essential unity that binds us all.

In navigating the depths of these universal truths, we are invited to transcend the limitations of our individual perspectives and embrace a broader, more inclusive understanding of our place in the cosmos. By recognizing the interconnectedness of all beings, the impermanence of all things, and the transcendent nature of reality itself, we can cultivate a profound sense of unity, compassion, and wisdom that transcends the boundaries of culture, religion, and belief, uniting us in our shared humanity and spiritual journey towards greater understanding and enlightenment.

As we delve deeper into the exploration of these spiritual concepts, we come to understand that transcendence is not merely an abstract idea but a lived experience. It is in the moments of stillness and contemplation, when we quiet the chatter of our minds and open our hearts to the mysteries of existence, that we catch glimpses of the transcendent realm beyond our everyday reality. In these moments of connection to something greater than ourselves, we find solace, meaning, and a deeper sense of purpose that transcends the transient nature of our material existence.

Similarly, the recognition of impermanence serves as a poignant reminder of the fragility and beauty of life. It teaches us to let go of attachments, to embrace the flow of change, and to live with a sense of awe and wonder at the ever-changing tapestry of existence. By accepting the impermanence of all things, we free ourselves from the grip of fear and resistance, allowing us to fully engage with the present moment and appreciate the richness and complexity of the world around us.

In contemplating the concept of unity and oneness, we are challenged to look beyond the surface distinctions that divide us and to recognize the deep interconnectedness that binds all beings together. This recognition of unity is not merely a theoretical concept but a call to action, inspiring us to show compassion, empathy, and care for all living creatures, knowing that we are all part of the same intricate web of life. It is through cultivating a sense of unity and interconnectedness that we transcend the narrow confines of our egos and expand our hearts to embrace the vastness of the universe.

In conclusion, the exploration of transcendence, impermanence, and unity within diverse religious traditions offers us a profound insight into the fundamental truths that underpin our existence. By delving into these universal concepts with an open heart and a curious mind, we are able to glimpse the eternal, ever-changing nature of reality and our interconnectedness with all beings. Through embracing these truths and living in alignment with them, we find ourselves on a transformative spiritual journey of self-discovery, wisdom, and compassion that transcends the boundaries of individual belief systems and unites us in our shared quest for meaning and understanding in the vast tapestry of existence.

Navigating Spirituality in a Modern World

In a rapidly changing and interconnected world, the quest for spiritual fulfillment can seem daunting. With so many distractions and demands on our time and attention, it can be challenging to cultivate a sense of inner peace and connection to the divine. However, navigating spirituality in a modern world is not only possible but essential for our well-being.

One key aspect of navigating spirituality in a modern world is finding balance. It's important to carve out time in our busy schedules for spiritual practices that nourish our souls and bring us closer to the divine. This could be through meditation, prayer, mindfulness, or simply spending time in nature and connecting with the world around us.

Balancing the demands of modern life with spiritual practice can be a delicate dance. In a world driven by productivity and achievement, it can be easy to neglect our spiritual well-being in favor of external success. However, true fulfillment comes not from material achievements alone but from a deep, inner connection to something greater than ourselves.

Another essential aspect of navigating spirituality in a modern world is grounding ourselves in our values and beliefs. In a culture that often values consumerism and individualism, it can be challenging to live in alignment with our spiritual principles. By reflecting on what truly matters to us and aligning our actions with our deepest values, we can find a sense of purpose and meaning that transcends the superficialities of modern life.

Staying true to our spiritual path also requires a willingness to engage with different perspectives and wisdom traditions. The world is rich with diverse spiritual practices and belief systems, each offering unique insights into the nature of the divine. By approaching other traditions with an open heart and mind, we can expand our understanding of spirituality and deepen our own connection to the sacred.

Moreover, in the modern world, technology and social media play a significant role in shaping how we experience spirituality. While these tools can offer access to vast amounts of spiritual knowledge and teachings, they can also be sources of distraction and disconnection. Finding a healthy balance in how we engage with technology and social media is essential for maintaining a strong spiritual practice.

Additionally, the challenges and complexities of the modern world can serve as opportunities for spiritual growth and transformation. By facing adversity with grace and resilience, we can deepen our spiritual understanding and cultivate a sense of inner strength and peace. Through mindfulness and self-reflection, we can navigate the ups and downs of life with greater ease and equanimity.

Ultimately, navigating spirituality in a modern world is about cultivating a sense of inner peace and connection that sustains us through life's challenges. It's about recognizing the interconnectedness of all beings and living with compassion and empathy towards ourselves and others. By continually exploring our spiritual path, seeking wisdom from diverse sources, and staying true to our values, we can navigate the complexities of the modern world with grace and integrity, finding true fulfillment and purpose in the process.

Cultivating a Personal Relationship with the Divine

In the sacred embrace of solitude, where the song of silence echoes through the chambers of our souls, we are enveloped in a divine stillness that transcends all earthly distractions and beckons us to journey deeper into the heart of existence. This profound space of inner sanctuary is a cosmic portal through which we can access the limitless potential of our true selves and connect with the boundless wisdom that flows from the eternal source of creation.

As we surrender to the gentle hush of solitude, we open ourselves to receive the sacred alchemy of transformation that occurs when we release the grip of the ego and allow our spirits to soar free. In this state of pure presence, we discover a wellspring of inspiration that nourishes our creativity and ignites the spark of divine purpose within us, propelling us to new heights of expression and realization.

The mystical dance of communion with the divine invites us to transcend the limitations of the material world and enter into a realm of pure consciousness where the barriers of time and space dissolve into the eternal now. In this timeless expanse, we are invited to partake in the cosmic symphony of creation, harmonizing our individual melodies with the universal chorus that reverberates throughout the cosmos.

Through the sacred practices of prayer, meditation, and contemplation, we cultivate a sacred dialogue with the divine presence that dwells within and around us, weaving a tapestry of connection that binds us to all living beings and the heartbeat of the universe. As we attune ourselves to the rhythms of the cosmic dance, we become channels through which the light of divine love flows into the world, radiating peace, harmony, and healing to all who cross our path.

In the depths of our inner sanctuary, we discover a well of resilience and inner strength that sustains us through the storms of life and guides us through the darkest nights of the soul. It is in these moments of solitude and stillness that we find solace in the arms of the divine, knowing that we are cradled in the loving embrace of a cosmic intelligence that transcends all understanding and guides us with infinite grace.

May we continue to deepen our communion with the divine, allowing its wisdom and love to permeate every fiber of our being and illuminate our path with the light of truth and compassion. In the sacred embrace of solitude, may we find the courage to surrender to the divine will and become radiant beacons of divine love in a world in need of healing and transformation. Amen.

Embracing Sacred Practices from Different Faiths

In a world where the rhythms of life often seem overwhelming and the mysteries of existence loom large, the pursuit of spiritual connection and insight becomes a vital anchor for the human soul. Across the globe, in every corner of the Earth, diverse faith traditions have blossomed, each offering a unique pathway to the divine and a profound way of understanding the mysteries of existence.

From the ancient Vedic hymns of Hinduism that resonate with the cosmic vibrations of the universe to the intricate sand mandalas of Tibetan Buddhism that symbolize the impermanent nature of reality, sacred practices serve as portals through which the human spirit can transcend the limitations of the material world and commune with the ineffable essence of existence.

The Sufi dervishes whirl in ecstatic trance, merging with the divine through the spiraling dance of love and surrender. The Native American sweat lodge ceremonies cleanse the body and spirit, forging a deep connection with the earth and the spirits of the land. The Jewish prayers at the Wailing Wall in Jerusalem carry the weight of centuries of longing and hope, a testament to the enduring faith of a people who have faced countless trials and tribulations.

In the solemn rituals of the Catholic Mass, the faithful partake in the mystical communion of body and blood, symbolizing the eternal bond between humanity and the divine. The chants of the Zen monks echo through the misty mountains of Japan, inviting practitioners to enter into silent communion with the true nature of reality. The animistic rituals of indigenous tribes around the world honor the spirits of nature and the ancestors, weaving a tapestry of connection that transcends time and space.

As we immerse ourselves in the rich tapestry of sacred practices from different faith traditions, we discover a common thread that unites all of humanity – the yearning for transcendence, the quest for meaning, and the search for connection with the divine. In the shared experience of sacred rituals and ceremonies, we find a reflection of our own spiritual journey, a reminder that we are all pilgrims on the path of awakening.

By exploring the depths of these sacred practices, we open ourselves to profound transformation and inner growth. We learn to embrace the diversity of human spiritual expression, recognizing that each tradition offers a unique perspective on the mysteries of existence and a valuable insight into the nature of the divine.

Through the practice of sacred rituals from different faith traditions, we cultivate a sense of reverence for the interconnectedness of all life and a deep respect for the wisdom that dwells within each tradition. We come to realize that beneath the surface diversity of religious practices lies a shared longing for unity, love, and transcendence – a universal language of the soul that transcends the boundaries of culture, language, and belief.

As we journey through the sacred practices of the world's faith traditions, we are called to honor the beauty and complexity of human spirituality, to embrace the wisdom of the ages, and to cultivate a spirit of openness, curiosity, and reverence for the mysteries of existence. In the tapestry of sacred practices from different faiths, we find a mirror reflecting the boundless expanse of the human spirit and the eternal presence of the divine.

Overcoming Fear and Guilt in Spiritual Discovery

In the intricate tapestry of spiritual exploration, the interplay between fear and guilt often serves as a profound crucible through which individuals navigate the depths of their inner selves. Fear, with its tendrils reaching into the unknown, can paralyze and confound even the most ardent seeker. It is the fear of rejection, of being misunderstood, that can sow doubt in the fertile soil of the soul. It is the fear of letting go, of relinquishing control to forces beyond our comprehension, that can stir unease in the most steadfast hearts.

And yet, it is precisely in these moments of trepidation that the true test of faith emerges. For it is in the act of stepping boldly into the murky waters of uncertainty that we begin to awaken to the vast potential that lies dormant within us. It is in facing our fears with unwavering resolve, with a spirit unbound by limitation, that we can transcend the confines of the mundane and soar into the realm of the divine.

Guilt, too, plays a formidable role in the spiritual odyssey. It is the weight of past misdeeds, of perceived wrongs, that can anchor us to the shores of regret and self-reproach. It is the guilt of not living up to societal expectations, of straying from the prescribed path, that can cast a shadow over the brightest of intentions. And yet, it is in the act of embracing our imperfections, of acknowledging our mistakes with humility and grace, that we can begin to unshackle ourselves from the chains of guilt and move towards a state of inner reconciliation.

Self-compassion, that balm for the wounded soul, emerges as a potent salve in the journey of spiritual discovery. By treating ourselves with gentleness and understanding, by extending the same compassion to ourselves that we would to a beloved friend, we can begin to dismantle the walls of fear and guilt that inhibit our growth. Through practices of mindfulness, meditation, and self-reflection, we can delve into the recesses of our being, shedding light on the shadows that dwell within and illuminating the path towards wholeness and self-realization.

In the grand tapestry of spiritual evolution, fear and guilt are but threads woven into the fabric of our existence. By embracing these emotions as integral aspects of our journey, by confronting them with courage and compassion, we can forge ahead on the path towards enlightenment and self-discovery. May we navigate the labyrinth of our inner landscapes with steadfastness and grace, knowing that through the crucible of fear and guilt, we emerge transformed and illuminated, ready to embrace the boundless potential that awaits us.

In this sacred dance of self-discovery, fear and guilt act as mirrors reflecting the deepest recesses of our souls. They beckon us to dive into the murky waters of our subconscious, to confront the shadows that linger in the corners of our being. Fear, with its primal instinct for self-preservation, whispers caution in our ears as we teeter on the edge of transformation. It is the fear of the unknown, of uncertainty and vulnerability, that can serve as a potent catalyst for growth if met with courage and resilience.

Similarly, guilt, that heavy cloak of past transgressions, weighs upon our shoulders like a burden we cannot shake. It is the guilt of missed opportunities, of unfulfilled promises, that can haunt our waking moments and dim the light of our spirit. And yet, it is in the act of embracing our humanity, of recognizing that we are fallible beings on a journey of evolution, that we can begin to release ourselves from the chains of guilt and move towards a state of profound acceptance and forgiveness.

Through the alchemical process of self-exploration and introspection, we come to understand that fear and guilt are not enemies to be vanquished but rather allies to be embraced. They serve as signposts along the path of self-realization, guiding us towards hidden truths and uncharted territories within ourselves. By delving into the depths of our fears and confronting the ghosts of our past actions, we unveil the raw essence of our being, stripped of pretense and ego.

In this sacred quest for inner illumination, we learn to dance with fear and guilt as partners in the intricate choreography of self-discovery. We come to see them not as barriers to our growth, but as gateways to deeper understanding and transformation. As we navigate the twists and turns of our inner landscapes, may we do so with grace and humility, knowing that through the crucible of fear and guilt, we emerge reborn, ready to embrace the fullness of our divine potential.

Living Authentically in Alignment With Your Truth

As we journey through the labyrinth of life, we are often met with a myriad of expectations, both external and internal. Society, culture, religion, and even our own minds can shape and mold us into someone we think we should be, rather than who we truly are. It takes courage and self-awareness to strip away these layers of conditioning and stand in our own truth.

Living authentically means embracing all parts of ourselves – the light and the shadow, the strengths and the vulnerabilities. It requires a deep sense of self-acceptance and a willingness to be vulnerable and honest with ourselves and others. When we live authentically, we no longer feel the need to wear masks or put on a façade to fit in or please others. We show up as our genuine selves, unapologetically and boldly.

Aligning with our truth means honoring our values, beliefs, and passions, even if they may go against the grain of societal expectations. It means listening to the whispers of our intuition and following the guidance of our inner compass, even when it leads us down unconventional paths. Living in alignment with our truth requires us to be in tune with our deepest desires and aspirations, and to take intentional actions that are in harmony with our authentic selves.

It is not always easy to live authentically. It can be a challenging and sometimes lonely road, as we may face criticism, judgment, and resistance from those around us. However, the reward of living in alignment with our truth is a deep sense of inner peace, fulfillment, and freedom. When we are true to ourselves, we attract people and opportunities that resonate with our authenticity, and we create a life that is a true reflection of who we are at our core.

In the journey of living authentically in alignment with our truth, we must continually reflect, reassess, and realign ourselves with what is most important to us. It is an ongoing process of self-discovery and self-expression, a journey of unraveling layers of conditioning and stepping into the fullness of our being. It is a courageous act of self-love and self-empowerment, and it is a journey worth taking for the sake of our own happiness and well-being.

Living authentically also means being open to growth and change. As we navigate the complexities of life, we must remain flexible and adaptive, willing to evolve and expand our understanding of ourselves and the world around us. This process of growth requires us to challenge our preconceived notions and beliefs, to be open to new perspectives and experiences, and to embrace the discomfort that often comes with personal transformation.

At the core of living authentically is the concept of self-awareness. By cultivating a deep understanding of ourselves – our values, motivations, fears, and desires – we can make conscious choices that align with our truest selves. Self-awareness allows us to recognize when we are veering off course and to course-correct with compassion and mindfulness. It is through this ongoing practice of self-reflection and introspection that we deepen our connection to our authentic nature and live a life that is aligned with our highest truth.

In essence, living authentically is a profound act of self-discovery and self-expression. It is a journey of embracing our uniqueness, celebrating our imperfections, and honoring the sacred essence of who we truly are. When we have the courage to live in alignment with our truth, we invite greater joy, fulfillment, and meaning into our lives. It is a path that beckons us to step into our power, to reclaim our voice, and to shine brightly as the radiant beings that we are.

When you shine brightly, you give others permission to shine with you. Joy is your birthright. Freedom is your birthright. Claim them and live your truth.
— Gabby Bernstein

CHAPTER 9

Living With Joy

The Joyful Mindset

In a world filled with challenges and uncertainties, cultivating a joyful mindset can be a powerful tool for navigating life with grace and resilience. A joyful mindset goes beyond mere positivity; it is a profound way of being that transcends momentary emotions and anchors us in a state of inner peace and contentment. It is a conscious choice to focus on the beauty and blessings that surround us, even in the midst of chaos and turmoil.

Mindfulness, a cornerstone of a joyful mindset, invites us to embrace the present moment with open-hearted awareness. By grounding ourselves in the now, we can let go of regrets about the past and fears about the future, allowing us to fully experience the richness of life as it unfolds. This practice of mindfulness not only deepens our connection to ourselves but also fosters a sense of interconnectedness with the world around us.

Self-compassion, another essential element of a joyful mindset, requires us to treat ourselves with the same kindness and understanding that we would offer to a dear friend. It involves acknowledging our humanity, with all its imperfections and vulnerabilities, and embracing our innate worthiness and dignity. By extending compassion towards ourselves, we can cultivate a sense of inner resilience and self-love that serves as a wellspring of joy and strength.

A joyful mindset also entails cultivating a sense of gratitude for the blessings in our lives. Gratitude is a transformative practice that shifts our focus from scarcity to abundance, from complaint to appreciation. When we approach life with a grateful heart, we open ourselves up to receiving more blessings and opportunities, as our positive energy attracts more positivity into our lives.

Moreover, a joyful mindset empowers us to find happiness from within, rather than seeking it from external sources. It liberates us from the endless pursuit of validation and approval from others, as we come to recognize that true happiness arises from a deep sense of self-acceptance and self-validation. This inner sense of joy and fulfillment becomes a guiding light that illuminates our path through life's twists and turns, providing us with the resilience and courage to face whatever challenges may come our way.

In embracing a joyful mindset, we embark on a transformative journey of self-discovery and empowerment. It is a path of awakening to the beauty and wonder that exists within and around us, of opening our hearts to love and compassion, and of finding meaning and purpose in the fabric of existence. As we walk this path with grace and gratitude, we become beacons of light, radiating joy and inspiration to all those we encounter on our shared journey of life.

Fun-Filled Adventures Await

Amidst the hustle and bustle of everyday life, there is a call for adventure that tugs at our souls. It beckons us to break free from routine and seek out new experiences that ignite our sense of wonder and curiosity. Fun-filled adventures await, promising thrills and memories that will last a lifetime.

Imagine embarking on a spontaneous road trip with friends, the wind in your hair and the open road stretching out before you. Every turn holds the promise of discovery, whether it be a hidden gem of a town or a breathtaking natural wonder. The thrill of the unknown fuels your excitement as you embrace the journey ahead.

Or perhaps your adventure leads you to the great outdoors, where the beauty of nature surrounds you in all its grandeur. Hiking through lush forests, camping under a blanket of stars, and immersing yourself in the sights and sounds of the wilderness awaken a sense of awe and reverence for the world around you.

Even within the confines of city life, there are adventures waiting to be had. Exploring vibrant neighborhoods, trying new cuisines, attending cultural events, and engaging in local activities can broaden your horizons and inject a sense of vibrancy into your routine.

The key to embracing fun-filled adventures is to approach them with an open mind and a willingness to step outside of your comfort zone. Allow yourself to be guided by spontaneity and curiosity, and you may find that the most memorable experiences often arise when you least expect them.

So embrace the call of adventure, dear reader, and let the thrill of the unknown propel you towards new and exciting horizons. Fun-filled adventures await, ready to spark joy and ignite your spirit of exploration.

As you venture forth into the unknown, remember that each new experience has the potential to shape and enrich your life in meaningful ways. Whether it's navigating uncharted paths, immersing yourself in unfamiliar cultures, or simply taking a moment to appreciate the beauty of the world around you, every adventure offers a chance for growth and self-discovery.

Embrace the challenges that come your way, for they are opportunities in disguise. Embrace the people you meet along your journey, for they may become lifelong friends or sources of inspiration. And most importantly, embrace the moments of pure joy and wonder that arise when you least expect them, for they are the true treasures of any adventure.

So go forth with courage and curiosity, and let the spirit of adventure guide you towards a life filled with excitement, fulfillment, and endless possibilities. The world is your playground, waiting to be explored and embraced in all its beauty and complexity. Enjoy the journey, dear reader, for the adventures that await are as limitless as your imagination.

Cultivating Everyday Happiness

In this chapter, we delve into the profound ways in which you can enhance and sustain happiness in your everyday life. True happiness is not a destination to reach but a continuous journey of self-discovery and contentment. By nurturing your inner world and practicing mindfulness, gratitude, and self-care, you can create a solid foundation for lasting happiness.

Gratitude is a potent force that can transform your outlook on life. When you cultivate a sense of gratitude, you shift your focus from what is lacking to what is abundant in your life. Keeping a gratitude journal, where you write down things you are thankful for each day, can help you reframe your perspective and cultivate a deeper appreciation for the blessings that surround you.

Mindfulness is a practice that invites you to fully engage with the present moment. By bringing your awareness to the here and now, you can savor the beauty and richness of life that is often overlooked in the hustle and bustle of daily living. Mindfulness allows you to observe your thoughts and feelings without judgment, fostering a sense of inner peace and acceptance.

Self-care is a non-negotiable aspect of maintaining happiness and well-being. Taking time to prioritize your physical, mental, and emotional health is essential for living a fulfilling life. Engage in activities that nourish your soul, whether it's practicing meditation, spending time in nature, or connecting with loved ones. Remember to set boundaries and prioritize your needs to prevent burnout and maintain a healthy balance in your life.

Incorporating these practices into your daily routine can lead to a profound shift in your overall happiness and satisfaction with life. By cultivating gratitude, practicing mindfulness, and prioritizing self-care, you can create a life that is rich in joy, peace, and fulfillment. Embrace the journey of everyday happiness with an open heart and a commitment to self-discovery and growth.

Furthermore, it is essential to recognize that happiness is not a static state but a dynamic interplay of various factors in your life. It is influenced by your thoughts, beliefs, relationships, and overall lifestyle choices. By fostering a positive mindset and surrounding yourself with supportive and uplifting individuals, you can create a harmonious environment that nurtures your happiness and well-being.

Embrace the power of positive thinking and affirmations to rewire your brain for happiness. Your thoughts and inner dialogue play a significant role in shaping your perception of the world and your emotional experiences. Practice replacing negative self-talk with positive affirmations that empower and uplift you. Affirmations such as "I am deserving of happiness" and "I choose to see the good in every situation" can shift your mindset towards a more optimistic and resilient outlook on life.

Additionally, incorporating mindfulness practices such as meditation and deep breathing exercises can help you cultivate inner peace and emotional resilience. Mindfulness allows you to observe and acknowledge your thoughts and feelings without attaching judgment or significance to them. By developing a sense of present-moment awareness, you can effectively manage stress, anxiety, and other negative emotions that may hinder your happiness.

In conclusion, happiness is not a destination to reach but a journey to embrace with an open heart and a mindful spirit. By cultivating gratitude, practicing mindfulness, prioritizing self-care, fostering positive relationships, and embracing the power of positive thinking, you can create a life that is abundant in joy, contentment, and fulfillment. Embrace the beauty of the present moment and savor the richness of life's experiences as you navigate your unique path towards lasting happiness.

Discovering Your Joyful Passions

As you journey through life, it is essential to explore and discover the things that bring you joy. Often, we get caught up in the busyness of everyday life and forget to nurture our passions. However, taking the time to identify and pursue activities that light up your soul can have a profound impact on your overall well-being.

To begin discovering your joyful passions, start by reflecting on what activities or hobbies make you feel truly alive. Consider the moments in your life where you felt most at peace, most authentically yourself. This introspection can bring valuable insights into what truly brings you joy. It could be anything from painting to hiking to cooking to playing music. Pay attention to the activities that make time fly by and leave you feeling energized and fulfilled.

Sometimes, our passions may lie dormant within us, waiting to be rediscovered. It's important to reconnect with your inner child and remember the things that brought you immense joy and excitement in the past. This could be a clue to uncovering your true passions and reigniting that spark within you.

As you explore different activities, don't be afraid to try new things and step out of your comfort zone. Embrace the discomfort of the unknown and trust that it is part of the journey towards self-discovery. Engaging in new experiences can broaden your perspective and open up new realms of possibility for joy and fulfillment.

It's important to remember that passions can evolve and change over time. What once brought you joy may no longer resonate with you, and that's okay. Allow yourself the freedom to explore new avenues and interests, staying open to the endless possibilities that life has to offer.

By prioritizing your passions and making time for them in your daily life, you are actively investing in your own well-being and happiness. Your passions are a reflection of your true self, the essence of who you are. Nurture them, cultivate them, and allow them to guide you towards a life filled with purpose, meaning, and fulfillment. Embrace the beauty of exploring your passions and let them light the way to a more enriched and joyful existence.

Embracing Playfulness in Life

Life is a beautiful dance of moments, each one offering an opportunity to embrace the joy of playfulness. In a world that often feels weighed down by responsibilities and expectations, cultivating a sense of light-heartedness can be a powerful antidote. Playfulness is not just about silliness or frivolity; it is a mindset that allows us to navigate the complexities of life with grace and creativity.

When we approach challenges with a playful spirit, we open ourselves up to new perspectives and solutions that may have been hidden to us before. Playfulness encourages us to take risks, to push past our comfort zones, and to experiment with different ways of being in the world. It is through playfulness that we can tap into our innate creativity and resourcefulness, paving the way for innovation and growth.

Moreover, playfulness is a key ingredient in fostering strong, meaningful relationships. When we engage with others in a playful manner, we create bonds built on mutual understanding and shared joy. Playfulness allows us to let down our guards, to be vulnerable and authentic, leading to deeper connections and a sense of community.

In a world that can often feel heavy and serious, embracing playfulness is a radical act of self-love and liberation. It is a reminder that life is meant to be enjoyed, that laughter and fun are not frivolous distractions but essential elements of a fulfilling existence. So let go of your inhibitions, embrace your inner child, and dance through life with a sense of playfulness that lights up your path and inspires those around you.

As we journey through the tapestry of life, we come to understand that playfulness is not just a fleeting emotion but a fundamental attitude that can transform the way we engage with the world. It is a lens through which we can see beauty in the mundane, find joy in the everyday, and approach challenges with a sense of curiosity and wonder. Playfulness allows us to release the grip of perfectionism and embrace the messiness of life with open arms, knowing that it is in the spontaneous, unscripted moments that true magic unfolds.

Furthermore, playfulness is a powerful tool for personal growth and self-discovery. By stepping outside our comfort zones and embracing the unknown, we invite opportunities for growth and expansion. Playfulness encourages us to trust in our instincts, to follow our intuition, and to explore the infinite possibilities that lie before us. It is through playfulness that we can break free from the constraints of fear and doubt, stepping boldly into our potential and unlocking hidden talents and strengths.

In essence, playfulness is a gateway to living a life of abundance and fulfillment. It is a reminder that we are not defined by our circumstances or limitations but by the boundless spirit of creativity and joy that resides within us. So, let us continue to dance through life with a playful heart, embracing all that comes our way with a sense of wonder and gratitude. Let us remember that playfulness is not just a choice but a way of being, a guiding light that illuminates our path and infuses each moment with warmth and vitality.

Creating Joyful Connections

Human beings are inherently social creatures, wired to seek out connection and belonging with others in various forms. Our relationships with friends, family, colleagues, and even strangers play a pivotal role in shaping our emotional experiences and sense of self. By cultivating meaningful and joyful connections, we can enrich our lives in countless ways.

To truly forge joyful connections, it is essential to engage in authentic and open communication with those around us. Authentic communication involves not only expressing ourselves honestly but also actively listening and showing empathy towards others. By developing a deep sense of understanding and empathy, we can nurture genuine connections that sustain and uplift us.

Kindness, compassion, and gratitude are powerful tools in strengthening the bonds we share with others. By approaching our relationships with a generosity of spirit and a willingness to support and uplift those we care about, we can create a positive and affirming environment that fosters joy and connection.

Spending quality time with loved ones, engaging in shared activities, and celebrating moments of joy together are all integral aspects of nurturing joyful connections. These shared experiences not only deepen our bonds but also create lasting memories that contribute to our overall sense of happiness and fulfillment.

In a society that often glorifies individualism and self-sufficiency, it is crucial to remember the immeasurable value of human connection.

Our relationships with others serve as a cornerstone of our emotional well-being and can provide us with solace, support, and companionship in both good times and bad. By prioritizing and nurturing joyful connections, we can cultivate a network of relationships that bring us a profound sense of joy and belonging.

Additionally, research has shown that individuals with strong social connections tend to experience better physical and mental health outcomes. Studies indicate that people with robust social networks are more resilient in the face of adversity, have lower levels of stress, and are at a reduced risk of developing mental health disorders like depression and anxiety.

Furthermore, joyful connections can positively impact not only our individual well-being but also our communities and society at large. When we cultivate a culture of kindness, empathy, and support within our social circles, we contribute to building a more compassionate and harmonious world where individuals feel seen, heard, and valued.

In conclusion, nurturing joyful connections is not just a source of personal happiness but also a powerful force for creating a more connected and caring world. By investing in our relationships, practicing empathy and kindness, and celebrating the moments of joy we share with others, we can create a ripple effect of positivity and fulfillment that resonates far beyond our immediate circles.

Finding Bliss In Little Moments

In a world that never seems to slow down, where the demands of modern life constantly pull us in a thousand different directions, it can be all too easy to overlook the simple moments that have the power to bring us true happiness and peace. The key lies not in seeking out grand gestures or epic events, but in finding solace and joy in the small, seemingly insignificant moments that make up the tapestry of our daily lives.

It is in the quiet moments, the stillness before dawn breaks, or the hush of a snowfall blanketing the earth, that we can truly find ourselves. These moments, often fleeting and easily missed if we're not paying attention, hold within them a profound sense of wonder and beauty. It is in these moments that we can connect with our true selves, our innermost thoughts and desires, and find solace in the simplicity of just being.

Slowing down and practicing mindfulness is essential in finding bliss in the little moments. It requires a conscious effort to quiet the mind, to let go of the constant chatter and distractions that threaten to pull us away from the present moment. By taking a breath, a moment to pause and appreciate the beauty that surrounds us, we can learn to savor the sweetness of life in all its forms.

Gratitude is another essential tool in unlocking the joy of the little moments. By expressing gratitude for the small things – a kind word, a warm smile, a delicious meal – we can shift our focus from what is lacking in our lives to what is abundant and fulfilling. Gratitude allows us to see the world through a lens of abundance, to recognize the blessings that surround us each and every day.

Connecting with nature is also a powerful way to find bliss in the little moments. The natural world is a source of endless wonder and beauty, from the intricate patterns of a leaf to the vast expanse of the night sky. By immersing ourselves in nature, taking a walk in the woods or simply sitting in a park, we can tap into a sense of peace and harmony that is often elusive in our busy lives.

In the end, finding bliss in the little moments is about cultivating a mindset of presence, gratitude, and connection. It is about taking the time to slow down, to savor the small joys that make life worth living, and to appreciate the beauty that surrounds us each and every day. By embracing the simple moments, by finding joy in the seemingly mundane, we can unlock a profound sense of happiness and contentment that is always within our reach.

Furthermore, as we dive deeper into the essence of these small moments, we begin to realize that they are not just fleeting instances but fragments of a larger tapestry that weaves together the fabric of our lives. Each small moment holds within it a story, a lesson, a memory that shapes who we are and how we perceive the world around us. By paying attention to these small moments, by treasuring them and holding them close, we can gain a deeper understanding of ourselves and our place in the universe.

The beauty of finding bliss in the little moments lies in its ability to ground us in the present, to anchor us in a world that is constantly changing and evolving. In these moments, we are reminded of the preciousness of life, of the interconnectedness of all things, and of the simple joys that can bring light to even the darkest of days. By embracing the small moments, by letting them seep into our souls and fill us with gratitude and wonder, we can truly experience the richness and fullness of life in all its infinite beauty.

Letting Go of Negativity, Inviting Joy

Negativity is a pervasive force that can seep into every aspect of our lives if left unchecked. It has the power to cloud our judgment, dampen our spirits, and hinder our ability to experience true joy and fulfillment. Understanding the roots of negativity is essential in order to confront and overcome its hold on us.

At its core, negativity often stems from a place of fear and insecurity. When we feel threatened or uncertain, our minds instinctively latch onto negative thoughts as a means of protection. These thoughts can manifest as self-doubt, skepticism, or a general sense of pessimism towards the world. Over time, this ingrained negativity can become a habitual way of thinking, shaping our outlook on life and coloring our interactions with others.

Breaking free from the grip of negativity requires a deep level of introspection and self-awareness. It involves recognizing the ways in which our own beliefs and past experiences contribute to our negative mindset. By shining a light on these internal patterns, we can begin to unravel the tangled web of negativity that holds us back from experiencing true happiness.

Practicing mindfulness is a powerful tool in this journey towards releasing negativity. By staying present and attuned to our thoughts and emotions, we can begin to observe them without attaching judgment or significance. This practice allows us to create space between ourselves and our negative thought patterns, giving us the opportunity to choose a different, more positive perspective.

Gratitude, as a counterbalance to negativity, plays a crucial role in shifting our focus towards the good in life. When we cultivate a mindset of gratitude, we train our minds to seek out and appreciate the blessings, big and small, that surround us each day. This shift in perspective can have a transformative effect on our overall sense of well-being, opening us up to a world of abundance and possibility.

Surrounding ourselves with positive influences is equally important in combating negativity. The people we choose to spend time with, the media we consume, and the environments we inhabit all play a role in shaping our emotional landscape. By consciously selecting sources of positivity and inspiration, we create a supportive ecosystem that nurtures our growth and fosters a sense of joy and contentment.

In the end, the journey towards releasing negativity and embracing joy is a deeply personal one. It requires courage, patience, and an unwavering commitment to self-improvement. By facing our inner demons head-on, practicing mindfulness, cultivating gratitude, and curating a positive environment, we can unlock the door to a life filled with boundless happiness and profound fulfillment.

Savoring the Joy of Now

In a world filled with distractions and constant busyness, it can be all too easy to overlook the beauty and joy that surrounds us in the present moment. Life moves at a rapid pace, pulling us in a million different directions and leaving little room for pause and reflection. Yet, it is precisely in those moments of pause that we can discover the richness and depth of our experiences.

Savoring the joy of now is not just about being present in the moment but about truly immersing ourselves in the beauty and wonder that surrounds us. It is about developing a keen awareness of our senses, allowing us to fully engage with the sights, sounds, smells, tastes, and textures of the present moment. When we savor the joy of now, we are not just going through the motions of life; we are actively participating in it, embracing its fullness and richness.

It can be as simple as taking a moment to appreciate the sunlight streaming through the window, the sound of birds chirping outside, or the feeling of a warm cup of tea cradled in our hands. These small moments of joy, when savored and appreciated, can bring a sense of peace and contentment that transcends the chaos of our daily lives.

In a world that often values productivity and accomplishment above all else, savoring the joy of now offers us a precious opportunity to slow down, to reconnect with ourselves and the world around us, and to find gratitude in the simple pleasures that make life truly meaningful. So, let us not rush through life, always chasing the next goal or milestone. Instead, let us pause, breathe, and savor the joy of now, for it is in these moments of presence and mindfulness that we can find the true essence of happiness and fulfillment.

Embracing the present moment in all its fullness allows us to connect deeply with ourselves and the world around us. It is a practice of mindfulness that cultivates gratitude and awareness, enabling us to find joy and contentment in the simplest of experiences. When we savor the joy of now, we are not only living in the present, but we are also nourishing our souls and enriching our lives.

Let us remember that life is not just about the big milestones or accomplishments but about the everyday moments that make up the fabric of our existence. By savoring the joy of now, we can find peace in the midst of chaos, beauty in the ordinary, and meaning in the mundane. So, take a deep breath, look around you, and savor the joy of now – for it is in this moment, right here and right now, that true happiness can be found.

Service to others is the rent we
pay for our room here on earth.
— Muhammad Ali

CHAPTER 10

You Gotta Give Something Back

Embracing Your Purpose with Passion

In a world where the noise of everyday life often drowns out the whispers of our true calling, it becomes imperative to dive deep within ourselves to unearth the essence of our purpose. Embracing your purpose with unabashed passion is a journey of self-discovery and self-actualization that transcends the mundane and elevates your existence to a higher plane.

At the core of every individual lies a unique resonance, a melody that, when embraced and nurtured with fervor, harmonizes the symphony of life in a profound and beautiful way. When you align your actions with this melody, when you dance to the rhythm of your purpose with unwavering dedication, the universe, in its infinite wisdom, conspires to support and elevate you on your path.

Passion is the fire that ignites your purpose, the fuel that propels you forward with unwavering determination. It is the driving force behind your actions, infusing them with a sense of urgency and significance. When you operate from a place of passion, every moment becomes an opportunity to express your most authentic self, to radiate the light of your soul into the world.

Walking the path of purpose with passion is not without its challenges. It demands courage, resilience, and a willingness to confront the shadows that lurk within. It beckons you to step boldly into the unknown, to embrace discomfort as a catalyst for growth, and to forge ahead with unwavering faith in the journey ahead.

But the rewards of embracing your purpose with passion are profound and immeasurable. As you tap into the wellspring of your inner truth, you find yourself buoyed by a sense of purpose and direction that transcends the transient ups and downs of everyday life. Success, then, is not merely a destination but a natural byproduct of your alignment with your purpose and the passion that drives you.

Living with passion and purpose is also a practice in mindfulness and presence. It invites you to savor each moment, to cultivate gratitude for the beauty that surrounds you, and to remain open to the myriad possibilities that lie on the horizon. By anchoring yourself in the present moment, you unlock the transformative power of now and empower yourself to shape your reality with intention and grace.

Furthermore, embracing your purpose with passion requires a deep level of self-awareness and introspection. It necessitates a willingness to confront your fears, insecurities, and limiting beliefs, and to transmute them into stepping stones towards your highest expression. When you have the courage to look within, to embrace the totality of who you are, you unlock the keys to your own liberation and step into the fullness of your potential.

In the grand tapestry of existence, each individual thread of purpose and passion weaves a unique pattern that contributes to the rich tapestry of life itself. Your purpose is not just a personal quest but a cosmic dance in which you play a vital role, interwoven with the destinies of others in a grand symphony of interconnectedness and unity.

As you journey deeper into the realms of your purpose and passion, remember that you are not alone. The universe conspires in your favor, offering guidance, support, and synchronicities to illuminate your path and propel you towards your highest destiny. Trust in the unfolding of your journey, embrace the challenges as opportunities for growth, and let the flame of your passion illuminate the world around you.

Embracing your purpose with passion is a sacred act, a testament to your commitment to living a life of authenticity, meaning, and impact. It is a gift not only to yourself but to all those whose lives you touch, inspiring them to embark on their own journeys of self-discovery and self-realization. So, let your purpose be your guiding star, let your passion be your compass, and let your life be a radiant expression of your deepest truth.

Discovering Your Unique Gifts

In the exploration of one's unique gifts and talents, we uncover the essence of our individuality and the power we hold to make a difference in the world. Each person carries within them a set of innate abilities and strengths that, when nurtured and cultivated, can lead to a life of profound fulfillment and impact.

To truly understand and harness our unique gifts, it is essential to delve beneath the surface of our daily routines and societal expectations. This requires a deep level of introspection and self-awareness, allowing us to identify the aspects of ourselves that bring us joy, fulfillment, and a sense of purpose.

Our gifts often reveal themselves through activities that come effortlessly to us, where time seems to slip away and we are fully immersed in the moment. These moments of flow offer a glimpse into our unique talents and provide a pathway to unlocking our full potential.

Seeking feedback and guidance from others can also be a valuable part of this journey. Trusted friends, mentors, or coaches can offer fresh perspectives and insights that help us see ourselves more clearly. Their observations can shed light on aspects of our gifts that we may not have recognized on our own.

It is important to approach this process with a mindset of self-acceptance and celebration. Our gifts are what make us uniquely ourselves, and comparison to others only serves to diminish the beauty and value of our individual talents. Embracing our uniqueness and honoring our gifts allows us to fully step into our authenticity and create a life that is truly aligned with who we are meant to be.

By embracing and cultivating our unique gifts, we not only enrich our own lives but also have the potential to positively impact those around us. Our gifts are meant to be shared with the world, inspiring others and creating a ripple effect of positivity and growth. When we honor our gifts and allow them to shine brightly, we create a ripple effect that extends far beyond ourselves, shaping a world that is richer, more vibrant, and more deeply connected.

The Transformative Power of Service

In the chapter "The Transformative Power of Service," we delve into the intricate dynamics of service and its profound impact on both individuals and societies. Service, often regarded as a selfless act of helping others, goes beyond mere altruism; it is a fundamental expression of our shared humanity and interconnectedness.

At the heart of service lies the notion of empathy and compassion, the ability to understand and share the feelings of others. When we engage in acts of service, we not only provide material assistance but also demonstrate our solidarity with those in need. This shared sense of connection and support forms the groundwork for building resilient communities and fostering a culture of mutual aid.

The transformative power of service extends beyond the immediate impact of helping individuals in need. It serves as a catalyst for social change, challenging systemic inequalities and injustices. By advocating for marginalized communities and amplifying their voices, service becomes a tool for dismantling oppressive structures and promoting equity and justice for all.

Furthermore, engaging in service offers a profound opportunity for personal growth and self-reflection. By stepping outside of our own experiences and immersing ourselves in the realities of others, we confront our biases, assumptions, and privileges. This introspective journey not only deepens our understanding of the world but also sparks a process of transformation within ourselves, fostering empathy, humility, and a heightened sense of social responsibility.

Service is not merely a one-time act but a way of life, a philosophy that invites us to think beyond ourselves and consider the well-being of others. It challenges us to examine our values, beliefs, and actions, prompting us to strive for a more compassionate and just society. Through service, we tap into the collective power of individuals coming together with a common goal: to create a world where kindness, empathy, and solidarity are at the forefront of our interactions.

In essence, the transformative power of service lies in its ability to transcend boundaries, bridge divides, and cultivate a sense of interconnectedness among all beings. It is a reminder that our actions, no matter how small, have the potential to ripple outwards and shape a more compassionate and equitable world for generations to come.

Spreading Joy Through Acts of Kindness

In a world that can often feel dark and heavy, the simple act of kindness has the power to spread joy and light like wildfire. When we extend a helping hand or offer a kind word to someone in need, we not only uplift their spirits but also nourish our own souls.

Acts of kindness come in many forms, big and small. It could be something as simple as holding the door open for a stranger, complimenting a coworker on a job well done, or volunteering at a local shelter. The beauty of kindness is that it knows no boundaries – it transcends age, race, and background, connecting us all in a shared humanity.

When we make a conscious effort to spread joy through acts of kindness, we create a ripple effect that touches the lives of those around us. The recipient of our kindness is more likely to pay it forward, creating a chain reaction of positivity and goodwill.

In today's fast-paced world, it can be easy to get caught up in our own lives and forget the impact a simple act of kindness can have. But when we take the time to slow down, look around, and extend a helping hand to those in need, we not only make the world a better place but also fill our hearts with a deep sense of purpose and fulfillment.

Kindness is a universal language that speaks to the core of our humanity. It has the power to bridge divides and bring people together in a spirit of compassion and empathy. When we choose kindness, we not only make a difference in the lives of others but also strengthen our own moral character and sense of connectedness to the world around us.

So, let us all commit to spreading joy through acts of kindness, knowing that in doing so, we are not only making the world a brighter place but also nurturing our own souls in the process. Through the simple yet profound act of kindness, we have the ability to create a ripple effect of positivity that can truly change the world for the better.

When we choose kindness, we are not only benefiting others, but also ourselves. Research has shown that practicing kindness can lead to increased levels of happiness, reduced stress, and even improved physical health. When we engage in acts of kindness, our brains release oxytocin, often referred to as the "love hormone," which promotes feelings of love, connection, and trust.

It is important to remember that kindness is not solely about the recipient of our actions; it also deeply impacts our own well-being. By cultivating a habit of kindness, we are nurturing our own emotional resilience and fostering a sense of positivity and gratitude in our lives.

In a world that can sometimes feel cold and indifferent, kindness shines like a beacon of hope, reminding us of the beauty and potential for goodness that exists within each of us. Let us continue to spread kindness far and wide, knowing that in doing so, we are not only making the world a better place but also enriching our own lives in profound and meaningful ways.

Building Meaningful Connections

As human beings, our innate desire for connection and belonging is deeply intertwined with our overall well-being and sense of fulfillment. In a society increasingly marked by digital communication and virtual interactions, the importance of building meaningful connections in our lives has never been more paramount.

When we talk about meaningful connections, we are delving into the realm of genuine and profound relationships that transcend the superficial and transactional aspects of our social interactions. These connections are rooted in authenticity, vulnerability, and mutual respect, creating a space where individuals can truly be themselves without fear of judgment or rejection.

One key aspect of fostering meaningful connections is the practice of active listening. By actively engaging with others - not just hearing their words but truly understanding their emotions, intentions, and perspectives - we demonstrate a level of empathy and compassion that forms the cornerstone of deep relationships. Through active listening, we create a foundation of trust and understanding that paves the way for genuine connection.

Furthermore, meaningful connections are built on reciprocity and mutual support.

It is not simply about what we can gain from our relationships, but rather how we can contribute to the growth and well-being of others. By offering our time, attention, and genuine care to those around us, we sow the seeds of meaningful connections that can blossom into enduring bonds of friendship, love, and support.

In today's fast-paced and often fragmented world, the value of meaningful connections cannot be overstated. These connections provide a sense of belonging and community that transcends geographic boundaries and cultural differences. In times of need or celebration, they serve as a source of strength, solace, and joy, reminding us of the profound impact that human connection can have on our lives.

Moreover, research has shown that individuals with strong social support networks are more resilient in the face of adversity and experience greater levels of happiness and life satisfaction. Meaningful connections not only enrich our personal lives but also contribute to our mental and emotional well-being, underscoring the profound impact of authentic relationships on our overall quality of life.

In essence, the cultivation of meaningful connections is both an art and a science, requiring intentionality, empathy, and a willingness to be vulnerable. By investing in these deep bonds with others, we not only enhance our own lives but also contribute to a more compassionate, understanding, and interconnected society. As we continue to navigate the complexities of the modern world, let us never underestimate the transformative power of meaningful connections in shaping our collective human experience.

Cultivating Gratitude in Service

In a world filled with distractions and challenges, it can be easy to lose sight of the blessings that surround us every day. Cultivating gratitude in service is a powerful practice that can transform our outlook on life and deepen our connection to others.

When we approach our service with a mindset of gratitude, we open ourselves up to a greater sense of appreciation for the opportunities to make a difference in the lives of those around us. By acknowledging and celebrating the small victories and moments of joy that come from serving others, we can cultivate a sense of fulfillment that sustains us in our efforts.

Gratitude also allows us to shift our focus from what we lack to what we have, fostering a sense of abundance that motivates us to continue serving with a generous heart. When we express gratitude for the privilege of being able to help others, we not only uplift those we serve but also nourish our own spirits.

Furthermore, practicing gratitude in service can help us navigate the inevitable challenges and setbacks that may arise along the way. By focusing on the positive aspects of our work and the impact we are making, we can find the strength and resilience to overcome obstacles and persevere in our mission.

In essence, cultivating gratitude in service is not only a gift we give to others but also a gift we give to ourselves. It enriches our experience of serving others, deepens our connections with those we help, and nourishes our own well-being. Let us embrace gratitude as a guiding principle in our service and allow it to illuminate our path with light and warmth.

Gratitude in service is a transformative force that transcends individual actions and extends to the collective consciousness. When we embody gratitude in our service, we contribute to a ripple effect of positivity and kindness that reverberates throughout our communities.

Through the practice of gratitude, we acknowledge the interconnectedness of all beings and recognize the intrinsic value of each person we encounter. By expressing appreciation for the unique contributions and perspectives of those we serve, we foster a sense of inclusivity and unity that transcends boundaries and fosters a sense of belonging.

Moreover, gratitude in service serves as a beacon of hope in times of uncertainty and adversity. When we approach our service with a heart full of thankfulness, we not only uplift others but also inspire resilience and courage in the face of challenges. Gratitude becomes a source of strength that empowers us to persevere in our efforts and remain steadfast in our commitment to creating a better world for all.

In conclusion, cultivating gratitude in service is a profound act of love and selflessness that has the power to transform lives and uplift humanity. Let us embrace gratitude as a sacred practice in our service and allow it to guide us on a journey of compassion, connection, and transformation.

Finding Fulfillment in Giving Back

As we journey through life, we often seek fulfillment in various ways. Some find it in material possessions, others in personal achievements, but true fulfillment often comes from giving back to others. When we selflessly devote our time, energy, and resources to help those in need, we not only make a positive impact on their lives but also experience a deep sense of satisfaction and purpose within ourselves.

Giving back is a powerful way to connect with our communities and make a difference in the world around us. It goes beyond just the act of giving – it is an expression of empathy, compassion, and a recognition of our shared humanity. When we extend our hand to uplift others, we are fostering a sense of connection that transcends individual boundaries and unites us in a common goal of improving the collective well-being of society.

Volunteering at a local shelter, donating to a charitable cause, or engaging in random acts of kindness are all forms of giving back that have the potential to create a ripple effect of positivity and hope. By demonstrating care and concern for others, we not only brighten someone else's day but also inspire them to pay it forward and spread kindness to others in their own way.

In the act of giving back, we shift our focus from our own self-interests to the needs of those around us. It requires us to step outside of our own comfort zones, confront societal injustices, and actively work towards creating a more inclusive and compassionate world for all. Through such acts of service, we not only make a tangible difference in the lives of others but also challenge ourselves to be better, more empathetic individuals.

Finding fulfillment in giving back is a continuous journey of self-discovery and personal growth. It involves cultivating a mindset of abundance and gratitude, acknowledging the blessings we have been bestowed with, and using them to uplift others who may not be as fortunate. It is a reminder that true fulfillment comes not from what we accumulate for ourselves but from the positive impact we make in the lives of others.

In essence, giving back is a reflection of our deepest values and beliefs. It is a testament to our capacity for empathy, kindness, and social responsibility. When we commit ourselves to serving others, we not only bring light and hope into the world but also nurture a sense of purpose and meaning that transcends the boundaries of time and space. It is through these selfless acts of giving back that we truly embody the essence of humanity and contribute to the greater good of society.

Moreover, giving back also has a profound impact on our own mental and emotional well-being. Research has shown that altruistic acts release endorphins in the brain, which are hormones that promote feelings of happiness and overall well-being. By helping others, we not only make a difference in their lives but also experience a sense of fulfillment and joy that uplifts our own spirits.

Furthermore, giving back can foster a sense of connection and belonging within our communities. When we engage in acts of service and kindness, we create bonds with those around us and build a network of support that enriches our lives in profound ways. These connections can lead to lasting friendships, collaborations, and a sense of unity that transcends individual differences.

In today's fast-paced and often self-centered world, the act of giving back serves as a powerful antidote to feelings of isolation, apathy, and discontent. It reminds us of our interconnectedness with all beings and the importance of extending a helping hand to those in need. In embracing the spirit of generosity and empathy, we not only contribute to the well-being of others but also nurture our own souls and inspire others to follow suit in creating a more compassionate and caring world for all.

In conclusion, giving back is not just a noble gesture but a fundamental aspect of what it means to be human. It is through the act of selflessly serving others that we tap into our truest selves and make a lasting impact on the world around us. Let us continue to embody the spirit of giving back, for in doing so, we cultivate a legacy of kindness, compassion, and love that transcends time and space.

Inspiring Change Through Compassion

As a writer, my exploration of the transformative power of compassion delves even deeper into the intricate layers of human connection and empathy. In this extended section, you delve into the neuroscience behind compassion, shedding light on how acts of kindness can elicit profound emotional and physiological responses in both the giver and the recipient.

You uncover research that shows how practicing compassion can activate regions of the brain associated with empathy, love, and social bonding. Studies have demonstrated that individuals who engage in acts of compassion exhibit increased levels of oxytocin, commonly known as the "love hormone," which plays a crucial role in fostering feelings of trust, connection, and well-being. Furthermore, the act of giving has been shown to activate the brain's reward system, leading to feelings of happiness and fulfillment.

Drawing from psychology and sociology, you explore how compassion can shape our sense of identity and belonging. By promoting a sense of shared humanity and interdependence, acts of compassion have the potential to break down barriers and foster a more inclusive and empathetic society. Through understanding the interconnectedness of all beings, individuals can cultivate a deeper sense of purpose and meaning in their lives.

You also delve into the concept of compassion fatigue, acknowledging the emotional toll that can come from consistently giving to others. It is essential to practice self-care and set healthy boundaries when engaging in compassionate acts to prevent burnout and maintain emotional resilience. By prioritizing self-compassion and seeking support when needed, individuals can sustain their capacity to continue making a positive impact in the world.

The chapter expands on the cultural and historical significance of compassion, tracing its roots in ancient philosophies and religious teachings. From the Golden Rule found in various faith traditions to the concept of ahimsa in Hinduism and Buddhism, the notion of treating others with kindness and empathy has long been a central tenet of ethical principles across cultures. By tapping into these rich traditions and moral frameworks, individuals can draw strength and guidance in their practice of compassion.

Through a tapestry of scientific insights, psychological perspectives, and philosophical reflections, you invite readers to deepen their understanding of compassion as a force for healing and transformation. By integrating empathy, kindness, and acceptance into their daily lives, individuals can cultivate a more compassionate world—one where understanding, connection, and love reign supreme.

The Joy of Being in Service Every Day

As you wake up each morning, a sense of purpose fills your heart and mind. You find joy in the simple act of being able to serve others each day. It's not just about the tasks you accomplish or the goals you achieve; it's about the impact you make in the lives of those around you.

Every day presents new opportunities to make a difference, whether it's a kind word to a stranger, a helping hand to a friend in need, or a listening ear to someone going through a difficult time. The joy of service comes from the genuine connections you form with others, the sense of fulfillment from knowing that you've made a positive impact, no matter how small.

Being in service every day is not always easy. There are challenges and setbacks along the way, moments of doubt and moments of exhaustion. But through it all, you find strength in your purpose, in the knowledge that what you do matters, that your actions have the power to inspire change and bring hope to those who need it most.

In the depths of your soul, you feel a profound sense of gratitude for the opportunity to serve others. It is a privilege to be able to offer your time, skills, and compassion to those in need, to be a source of support and encouragement in a world that can sometimes feel overwhelming and isolating.

Through your service, you learn the true meaning of empathy and humility. You understand that everyone has their own struggles and challenges, and that a kind word or gesture can make a world of difference to someone in need. Your heart is open to the pain and joy of others, and you carry their stories with you as a reminder of the interconnectedness of all humanity.

As you continue on your journey of service, you realize that it is not just about what you give, but also about what you receive in return. The relationships you build, the connections you make, and the lessons you learn along the way enrich your own life in ways you never could have imagined. In serving others, you discover a deeper sense of purpose, a greater understanding of yourself, and a profound sense of fulfillment that transcends mere words.

So, as you embrace each day with a heart full of compassion and a spirit of generosity, remember the joy that comes from being in service every day. It is a gift you give to yourself and to the world, a reminder that we are all connected in our humanity, and that we can make a difference, one small act of kindness at a time.

About Coach Michael Taylor

Michael Taylor is a shining example of resilience and determination, having overcome immense personal challenges to become a renowned life coach, motivational speaker, and bestselling author. His unwavering commitment to empowering others has inspired countless individuals to pursue their dreams and live extraordinary lives.

A former high school dropout, Michael faced seemingly insurmountable obstacles, including divorce, bankruptcy, foreclosure, depression, and even homelessness. Yet, through sheer grit and an unshakable belief in himself, he emerged from these trials as a beacon of hope and inspiration.

With 14 published books under his belt, Michael's words have touched the lives of readers worldwide, guiding them towards personal growth, self-discovery, and the realization of their full potential. As a certified life coach, he has dedicated his life to helping men and women break free from self-imposed limitations and embrace the extraordinary within themselves.

Michael's journey has been a testament to the power of perseverance and the indomitable human spirit. As the president and CEO of Creation Publishing Group, he continues to champion the pursuit of dreams and the creation of a life filled with purpose and fulfillment.

Happily married to his soulmate, Bedra, for over two decades, Michael finds solace and joy in the simple pleasures of life. When he's not empowering others through his writing and coaching, you'll find him indulging in the soulful melodies of 70s and 80s music or immersing himself in the latest cinematic masterpieces.

With an infectious optimism and an unwavering passion for the impossible, Michael Taylor stands as a testament to the boundless potential that lies within each of us. He firmly believes that there has never been a better time to be alive on this planet, and his mission is to inspire others to embrace this belief and live their lives to the fullest.

www.coachmichaeltaylor.com

mtaylor@coachmichaeltaylor.com

713-565-0083